ART QUILTS
Made Easy

MW00637899

Art Quilts Made Easy

Landauer Publishing, www.landauerpub.com, is an imprint of
Fox Chapel Publishing Company, Inc.

Copyright © 2022 by Dr. Susan Kruszynski and
Fox Chapel Publishing Company, Inc.,
903 Square Street, Mount Joy, PA 17552.

All rights reserved. No part of this book may be reproduced,
stored in a retrieval system, or transmitted in any form
or by any means, electronic, mechanical, photocopying,
recording, or otherwise, without the prior written permission
of Fox Chapel Publishing, except for the inclusion of brief
quotations in an acknowledged review and the enlargement
of the template patterns in this book for personal use only.
The patterns themselves, however, are not to be duplicated
for resale or distribution under any circumstances. Any such
copying is a violation of copyright law.

Project Team
Managing Editor: Gretchen Bacon
Acquisitions Editor: Amelia Johanson
Editor: Sherry Vitolo
Designer: Mary Ann Kahn
Indexer: Nancy Arndt

Photo credits: Unless otherwise noted, all photography and
illustrations by Dr. Susan Kruszynski. The following images
are from Shutterstock.com: front matter, chapter opener, and
project opener background texture: Anucha Tiemsom; 32
bottom: Frank Wortmann.

ISBN 978-1-947163-87-4

Library of Congress Control Number: 2022938515

We are always looking for talented authors.
To submit an idea, please send a brief inquiry to
acquisitions@foxchapelpublishing.com.

Note to Professional Copy Services: The publisher grants
you permission to make up to six copies of any quilt patterns
in this book for any customer who purchased this book and
states the copies are for personal use.

Printed in China
25 24 23 22   2 4 6 8 10 9 7 5 3 1

This book has been published with the intent to provide
accurate and authoritative information in regard to the
subject matter within. While every precaution has been
taken in the preparation of this book, the author and
publisher expressly disclaim any responsibility for any
errors, omissions, or adverse effects arising from the use or
application of the information contained herein.

ART QUILTS
Made Easy

12 Nature-Inspired Projects with Appliqué Techniques and Patterns

Dr. Susan Kruszynski

Contents

Hear the Birches Whispering art quilt, 24" x 36" (61 x 91cm). Nature feeds my soul and much of my art quilting is inspired by it.

An Introduction to Art Quilting

Thank you for choosing *Art Quilts Made Easy* and for inviting me to teach you the skills of art quilting through creating these projects. My goal is to add value to your life with what I share. *Art Quilts Made Easy* will enhance your knowledge by answering the question, "What is an art quilt?" and will increase your skills by giving you easy steps to get you started in this beautiful quilting style.

I'm putting my background as a longtime educator to work and sharing the best of the best and most successful techniques of art quilting with my readers. You don't need to be an artist or know how to draw to be successful at creating an art quilt. With creativity, fabric, and the right tools, you'll be ready to get started. I'll teach you how to turn your inspiration into a design for an art quilt and how to plan and map these designs. I'll share some simple artistic rules and tips to consider and explain the basic tools you'll use and the step-by-step process from top to bottom. Finally, I'll show you some options for finishing your art quilt projects.

Following my steps to create a collage art quilt will allow you to learn some tips and techniques to make art quilting much easier. Creating the step-by-step projects in the latter part of the book, six animal projects and six floral projects, will allow you to practice and improve your techniques. You'll end up with the tools and knowledge you need to create, experiment, and develop your personal style.

Definitions

Art quilting is a relatively new form of quilting, and the terms used to describe art quilting can be a bit confusing. When people ask me what I do, I jump into teacher mode to start defining my artform. My long answer is, "I am a collage landscape art quilter in the categories of fiber arts or textile arts." My short answer is, "I'm an art quilter." But what exactly does that mean? The following definitions will be helpful as you continue working through the book.

Fiber Arts/Textile Arts—Fiber arts and textile arts are both basically fabric artwork; the terms are used interchangeably. Fiber art can be defined as fine art that uses textiles such as fabric, yarn, and natural or synthetic fibers. Techniques used can include quilting, embroidery, collage, knitting or crocheting, macramé, weaving, dyeing, or any other techniques involving textiles. Different types of fiber art quilting include horizontal stripes, confetti or impressionist, mosaic with tiny squares, and collage with various-sized pieces. If the art is based on textiles, it can be considered a fiber art.

Art Quilter—A quilter using both modern and traditional quilting techniques to create fabric artwork based on ideas and images rather than the repeated pattern of blocks found in traditional quilting.

Landscape Art or Landscape Art Quilting—Landscape art is a representation of natural scenery in art. The art may include mountains, water, fields, forests, flora, or fauna, and it may or may not include man-made structures or people. Landscape quilters use manufactured and hand-dyed fabrics. It is possible to add fabric painting and collaging techniques to produce a landscape art quilt. A pictorial quilt is another name for a landscape art quilt.

Collage—"Collage" comes from the Greek-based French word *coller*, meaning to "stick on" or "glue." Collages can be created from a wide range of materials, the most well-known being paper. For collages in art quilting, we use fabrics with fusibles applied to the backs of the

fabrics. The word "appliqué" is very similar to the word "collage." Appliqué also means to decorate with pieces of fabric to form pictures or patterns. However, in the quilting world, appliqué often refers to applying pieces of fabric with rolled edges.

The term collage is both a work of art (noun) and a technique (verb) that you actively do; I collage (verb) to make an art collage (noun). The definition I like best is from the Tate Galleries' website, www.tate.org.uk. A collage is defined as a "work of art in which pieces of paper, photographs, fabric and other ephemera are arranged and stuck down onto a supporting surface."

With this in mind, collage art quilting uses small pieces of fabric (raw-edged or sometimes folded) grouped together to form a quilt top. It is a form of fiber art that looks like painting with fabric because the layering process and the final result are similar. For the purposes of this book, think of collage art quilting as painting with raw-edged fabric.

Reaching Upward, **Panel #1 art quilt, 28" x 36" (71 x 91cm).
Landscape art quilting uses fabrics to create intricate scenes.**

Every day I wake up at 4:00 a.m. and run to my design room to explore new fabrics, techniques, and design ideas.

My Style of Art Quilting

Historically, most quilts were constructed for the purpose of usability. Variations of quilting patterns and methods for traditional quilting have been around for a lot longer than patterns and methods for creating collage art quilts. After a small bit of research, I found that there were some surges in creating art quilts in the 1950s and 1970s. This is not a book about the history of art quilts, however. I only mention it because when I started to make collaged landscape art quilts in 2014, I only found a handful of books I could purchase for reference and instruction. In my galleries, shows, and art quilting classes, people often comment that they are seeing and experiencing art quilting for the first time.

I love being in my design room creating art quilts! Since 2014, through almost daily creation and construction time spent exploring art quilting techniques, I have enhanced my skills and knowledge. Each time I teach a class, other quilters also share their tips and tricks with me. My style has developed from my passion for design exploration, my love of fabrics, and my unorthodox approach to learning new things. Since my retirement from education in 2014, I've been constantly working to perfect my creation techniques

A few of my longtime friends joined me when I taught my first practice class in 2016.

and my methods of teaching and sharing the joy of art quilting.

I taught my first practice class in July 2016, and I've taught at least one class every other week locally since summer 2017. My time in my design room feeds my soul, but I truly love the looks of accomplishment and self-pride on the faces of those in my classes.

So, after all that, what is my style of fiber art? Art quilters vary in the techniques they use, but my methods involve:

- "Painting" with fabric; each art quilt resembles a painting and is a totally unique work of art
- Pictorial quilting
- Improvisational design and creating without an original pattern to follow
- Interpreting ideas, feelings, scenes, or objects
- Sizes of art quilts that range from very small to very large
- Three layers building a quilt sandwich: (1) a cotton backing, (2) a piece of quilt batting or fusible fleece in the middle, and (3) a decorative top layer
- Collaging with fusible interfacing atop a background layer—applying small fabric pieces backed with adhesives
- Raw edges on each piece of top-layer fabric (not rolled under)
- Mostly cotton fabrics used for the quilt tops—some manufactured fabrics and some hand-dyed, some traditional quilting prints and some "landscape quilting" prints
- Using a basic home sewing machine for fussy machine stitching (not free motion, though it can be) with thread colors that accent the beauty of the fabric pieces and colors
- Different amounts of machine top stitching/ thread painting to enhance the piece
- Adding fabric paints or inks to achieve desired effects with color
- Trimming the art quilt with a rotary cutter for a raw-edged finish, sometimes adding a binding or sewing the art quilt into a wide border
- Often gluing art quilts to fabric-covered stretched art canvases for ease in hanging

There are three layers that make up a standard quilt sandwich for an art quilt.

I often use raw edges in my art to create more natural shapes for items like trees, leaves, plants, and flowers.

An example of some of the thread painting or "fussy stitching" I add to my art quilts.

Ensuring Art Quilting Success

Collage art quilting tends to look very difficult. The biggest hindrances we encounter when trying something new are usually not a lack of knowledge or lack of materials. Our major stumbling blocks are often mental.

Fear can get in the way—We usually feel apprehension and anxiety about trying something new. Art quilting will teach you a lot about your fears and how best to give your mind a creative space to be artistic. We expect a lot from ourselves and tend to want to "get it right" on the first try. A reassuring pottery teacher I once met used an analogy that went something like this: "Your piano teacher wouldn't expect you to play a piece from Bach or Beethoven on the first day of class, so you and I can agree not to expect a Michelangelo or a Van Gogh to start." Meaning don't expect a masterpiece on your first try! Taking risks is how you learn new skills. Bottom line: Will yourself to be a risk taker.

Sometimes we sabotage ourselves—What keeps you from engaging in actual creative time? When I'm unsure about how to solve a problem I've encountered with a project, I start engaging in avoidance activities. If I go out to get a cup of coffee, I take time to scour the sink while I'm in the kitchen. When I finally wander back into my design room, I'll notice a stack of fabric for another project that needs backing. Pretty soon my entire block of quilting time is gone. I engage in all manner of time-wasting activities while feeling guilty about the lack of forward movement on my main goal. When I notice this

The completed *October Twist* art quilt, 18" x 18" (45.7 x 45.7cm). Mounting an art quilt on a stretched art canvas provides a nice finish that makes it easier to display.

happening, I try to stop and ask myself a few questions to get back on track:

- Do I need to take a step back and allow my brain time for problem solving, or do I need to just dive in and try something new to see where it will take me?
- Do I need to stop and tidy my design area to give myself more room to create, or am I using that as a delaying tactic?
- Is a different design project calling me, and would I rather be working on a something else?
- What will free my mind and give me the space I need to create?

Sometimes problems present opportunities. Without the trouble I had with this piece, I wouldn't have tried adding ink, something that improved the finished work.

Don't forget to ask yourself when you get your best work done. We all have rhythms, and most of us know if we are morning people or night people. We know when we are most alert and energetic. Since I'm a morning person and design work takes a lot of concentration and energy, using early morning hours for my creative time achieves the most rewarding results. I plan early hours for intense design time and save afternoon hours for work that is more routine, like backing fabrics with adhesive, cutting battings and backings, or organizing materials. You can arrange your time to best suit you.

We see mistakes as failures—Learning this art form is very forgiving since it doesn't require exactness and mistakes can even turn into unexpected blessings. Learning comes from your successes *and* from your mistakes. Having to figure out how to solve a problem can result in some of your prettiest and most satisfying achievements. You'll experience false starts, hesitations, times you may need to walk away for a while, and times you may need to seek advice or suggestions. This book provides guidance on how to avoid or "fix" some common mistakes, but growth always requires discomfort. Art quilters often must make mistakes and work outside of their comfort zone to create amazing new things.

Working without a safety net can be daunting—In traditional quilting there are concrete, step-by-step patterns (safety nets) to follow. Art quilting does have some step-by-step procedures, but it's more improvisational in nature. You might want to page through the entire book (as a guide) before you get started, but I encourage you to just dive in. Select a project. Try working through it one step at a time. You may not always feel like you know exactly where you are going, but you should trust yourself, your tools, and the process. Art quilting is a journey, not a destination. In trying the projects, you'll gain the confidence and knowledge needed to design your own art quilts. Two promises: You will have fun and it is easier than it looks.

Reaching Upward, Panel #11, 28" x 36" (71.1 x 91.4cm). When creating art quilts, I always trust that the next step will appear. I "listen" to my materials, and these fabrics seemed to want to become water, earth, and autumn trees.

Chapter 2

My first art quilt wasn't perfect, but I loved how it captured my vision.

Here you can see the final art quilt images next to the original photo inspirations.

Kruszing Through the Seasons, each piece approximately 9" x 9" (22.9 x 22.9cm). The finished product combines all four pieces into a whole by adding fabric borders with additional fussy-cut details.

Design Inspiration

The first art quilts I ever saw showed beautiful shorelines. Soon after seeing them, my family and I decided we wanted to hang a new picture over the fireplace of our Saugatuck/Douglas Beach house. I knew I *needed* to create an art quilt of a land-and-water scene for this purpose. I had no idea what I was doing, assembled the art quilt in the hardest way possible, and would now call it a "Charlie Brown" attempt. Yet, I loved it! I loved the subject and the act of creating that first collaged art quilt.

After that first attempt, I made a beach scene from a tutorial in Ann Loveless's *Landscape Art Quilts, Step-by-Step,* which gave me some actual practical guidance for creating art quilts (thank you, Ann). It was all well and good to create an art quilt from someone else's tutorial, but I wanted to see if I could use some of these new skills to create more of my own art quilt designs. Here's where I had to

deal with the topic of inspiration. What was worthy of the time I would devote to creating more art quilts? What did I love enough? I knew I was always drawn to sets of scenes. Could I, perhaps, make art quilt scenes from each of the four seasons? I started searching for reference pictures. By searching the internet, I found pictures of a cardinal in a tree and a dahlia to inspire the winter and summer scenes. While scrolling Facebook, I saw photos of a spring trillium and a harvested field shared by Sandy Young, a local photographer. I requested and received permission to use Sandy's shots as inspirations for the spring and autumn scenes.

In these beginning steps on my journey as an art quilter, I hit on the useful technique of gathering inspirational reference pictures around me as I design an art quilt. That has been essential to creating more realism in my art quilts.

Inspiration: A gorgeous flower box outside Blueberry Haven in Grand Haven, Michigan.

Result: *Blueberries and Bliss* art quilt, 11" x 14" (27.9 x 35.6cm).

What can spark an idea for an art quilt?

- a scene in nature
- a photo in your own gallery
- a picture on an internet site
- a greeting card
- a piece of artwork
- a beautiful piece of fabric
- a story or a poem
- a social issue
- something close to the heart

Inspiration for an art quilt can begin with appreciating the beauty of a flower in the landscaping outside a business or a restaurant (snap a picture!) or in seeing a picture of a fall scene your friend posted on Facebook (ask to use it!). Perhaps a piece of fabric in a quilt shop catches your eye. The seed of an idea can start with a painting on the wall at the doctor's office. Germination begins. An idea for an art quilt is born. Visual representations like these spark the seeds for art quilts. Life can be breathed into an art quilt inspired by a story or a social issue. Something that touches your heart could point you toward wanting to turn that feeling into an art quilt. If you are deeply moved by a subject or a topic, that is a great inspiration for an art quilt. The following pages include a few examples from my own life and art quilting experience. They also outline some guiding steps that will allow you to visualize the things that stir you and develop them into art quilts.

Inspiration: A beautiful piece of vibrant teal fabric.

Result: *Touch of Teal on the Lakeshore* art quilt, 24" x 36" (61 x 91.4cm).

Inspiration: The impressive northern Napali coastline on the island of Kauai in Hawaii.

Result: *Napali Coast Kauai* art quilt, 11" x 14" (27.9 x 35.6cm).

Inspiration: When I saw this beautiful poppy fabric in a quilt shop, I purchased it, knowing it would be used in an art quilt someday in the future.

Result: *Red Poppies* art quilt, 18" x 24" (45.7 x 61cm).

Inspiration: My friend Kim's photo of rainy Las Vegas and a reference picture of a couple under an umbrella.

Result: *Las Vegas* art quilt, 16" x 20" (40.6 x 50.8cm).

Save Pictures of Your Favorite Subjects

- Take pictures of things that inspire you. In your electronic or physical photo gallery, create a folder labeled "Future Art Quilt Ideas."
- Collect pictures from books, magazines, or Facebook and save them in a folder, album, or in an electronic file.
- Create a spot in your work area for collecting seed ideas (pictures and pleasing fabrics) that might bloom into future projects.

How to Search for More Pictures

I may already have one picture of my subject, but more is better. To find additional reference pictures or to conduct a study on your topic, it's helpful to do an internet search. Try these steps for image searches:

- Open a search engine
- Type in a search term like "cattails"
- Click on "Image" to look at all the pictures
- Try including the word "painting" in your search (for example, "cattail painting")

Conduct a Study and Surround Yourself with Images

When I want to create a new art quilt, I have learned that using reference pictures or conducting a study on my subject is essential. In the world of art, a "study" is looking at your subject in real life or looking at drawings, sketches, pictures, or paintings of your subject. A study can include drawing, sketching, and taking notes in preparation for creating your piece of art.

You should also print the reference pictures that inspire you. When you are working on an art quilt, tape or clip your study and reference images to the wall. Surround your work area with these pictures.

I surrounded myself with reference and study pictures when creating my *Over the Cattails* art quilt.

To draw the human body artists are taught to study human anatomy. It stands to reason that if I want to capture the essence of a pumpkin in my fabric art, I should study pictures of pumpkins. Looking at a lot of pumpkin pictures will give me general ideas about the way an individual pumpkin appears. Research and pictures often serve as general inspiration. We want to keep copyright laws in mind while using references; we should not directly copy or imitate an artist's work and should only use the images we see for general ideas. Get permission from artists, use public domain sources, and never use photos or pictures without changing them in significant ways so that it is not copying. If I have done a study on the subject and have several pictures for reference during the design phase, my results are more pleasing and pumpkin-like as well as unique to me.

A pumpkin illustration I used as one of many reference images.

The pumpkin reference images were the inspiration for my own original sketch.

Result: *October Twist* art quilt, 18" x 18" (45.7 x 45.7cm).

Choose a size of art quilt—do you want to go super tiny, medium, or substantial?

Think Like an Artist—Plan Your Art Quilt

Once you've chosen an inspiring subject or a general concept for your art quilt, you must make a few more decisions regarding the overall layout and arrangement of the piece.

Choose the Medium (Cardstock or Fabric), Size, and Orientation

Medium (cardstock or fabric)—Usually, art quilts are made of fabric, but because I included a project using cardstock in this book, I will discuss information about that medium, as well.

Size—Whether you are making a fiber art scene on the front of a blank card or as a fabric-only art quilt, you need to choose the size of the finished piece. For blank cards, I suggest A2 cards—4¼" x 5½" (42 x 59.4cm) cardstock

Sometimes you will need to adapt a design by removing elements to make it work for a smaller format.

with envelopes—as a good place to start. For fabric-only art quilts, decide if you want to go **small or big**.

The smallest fabric art I ever made was probably created to fit on a 2" x 3" (5.1 x 7.6cm) art canvas. I commonly make bookmarks 2¼" x 7½" (5.7 x 19.1cm), and I make many other art quilts that fit on art canvases ranging in size from 3" x 5" (7.5 x 12.5cm) to 36" x 48" (90 x 120cm). The most commonly available art canvas sizes are listed in the Standard Art Canvas Sizes chart at right.

I also recently made six 40" x 60" (approx. 1 x 1.5m) art quilts (without standard canvas art frames) to illustrate a story and a queen-sized art quilt of a beach scene for my bed. I'll let you in on a secret, though: small art quilts are easier to make. A nice beginning size art quilt that is easy to handle and includes pieces that are not too small might be 8" x 10" (20.3 x 25.4cm) or even 16" x 20" (40.6 x 50.8cm).

Orientation—Should the orientation of the quilt be square or rectangular? If it's rectangular, should you go with a landscape or portrait orientation? It's a matter of what best fits your concept.

STANDARD CANVAS SIZES

INCHES	CENTIMETERS (APPROX.)
4" x 4"	10.2 x 10.2
5" x 3"	12.5 x 7.5
5" x 5"	12.5 x 12.5
6" x 4"	15 x 10.2
7" x 5"	17.5 x 12.5
8" x 8"	20 x 20
10" x 8"	25 x 20
10" x 10"	25 x 25
12" x 9"	30 x 23
12" x 12"	30 x 30
14" x 11"	35 x 30
16" x 12"	40 x 30
18" x 18"	45 x 45
18" x 24"	45 x 60
20" x 16"	50 x 40
20" x 20"	50 x 50
24" x 12"	60 x 30
24" x 36"	60 x 90
48" x 36"	120 x 90

Your subject should guide whether you choose a landscape or portrait orientation. Landscape orientation works well to frame wide scenes like the one on the right, and portrait orientation will highlight tall, single subjects like the bouquet on the left.

Create a Plan from Your Reference and Study Images

Sometimes just **one** inspiring photo or picture is enough to guide you when making a sketch or initial plan for your future art quilt. More often, you will have to use elements from **several** photos to create your design plan. Place your picture or pictures in front of you along with a piece of paper that is about the size and shape you've chosen for your art quilt.

I used just this one picture I took gazing upward under a tree as inspiration for an overall art quilt design.

The resulting piece, panel #4 from my *Reaching Upward* art quilt series, shows the view a young sapling would see when gazing up at an old pine tree.

I used this group of inspiration photos to answer a few questions: What does a stormy winter sky look like? How about snow on the side of a tree or piling around the bottom of a tree?

Panel #6 from my *Reaching Upward* art quilt series shows how I took my notes from the inspiration photos and applied them in fabric.

Sketch the Composition

In your sketch or drawing, include the composition, or components, of the major elements. For example, how wide is the sky or upper background area as compared to the lower area, and is the focal point more to the right or to the left? You can start with a very simple drawing like the sketch of one of my earliest winter scenes. Later you may decide to take the time to sketch another drawing that includes a few more specific details to calculate fabric dimensions.

Sometimes a sketch is unnecessary. A photo can take the place of a drawing if it happens to include the composition and design elements you want to include in the art quilt.

I made a detailed sketch for the layout of *Cardinal in the Oak*.

The resulting art quilt, *Cardinal in the Oak*, 12" x 16" (30.5 x 40.6cm), was very close to the original sketch.

A photo can take the place of a drawing or sketch as preparation for an art quilt. This older photo of the pasture on our sheep farm along the Pine River in Michigan has a great composition.

When I designed the finished quilt, *The Big Bend*, 18" x 24" (45.7 x 61cm), in 2020, I left the general layout much the same as the photo.

Design Rules, Guidelines, and Tips

Now is a good time in the early stages of designing your art quilt to consider some basic design rules, guidelines, and tips. As you work on the composition sketch for your art quilt, think about the following:

Rule 1—Keep your reference pictures near you as you design. I need physical reference pictures near me as I design so the elements in the art quilt will look realistic. Taping your reference pictures to a wall near your design space is one way to keep them from getting lost during the creative process.

Rule 2—Use the rule of thirds. The rule of thirds is a compositional strategy in which you divide your art surface horizontally or vertically into three equal sections to provide balance. An arrangement in thirds provides harmony and is an aesthetically pleasing formation. Think of this as a nine-patch grid. To achieve this balance, I often have three horizontal sections in an art quilt. For example, sky for the top third, a central element for the middle third, and a base for the bottom third. The technique of creating things with three parts is often used in landscape painting and photography, but can apply to any genre. As one of the beginning composition rules taught to artists, it's a quick and easy way for anyone, even beginners, to improve the visual impact of their work.

Even though my workspace might have looked chaotic during the design phase of my *Miss Dragonfly* art quilt, my reference pictures were always close by and easy to find.

The nine-patch grid overlaying the composition for this beach scene shows how it is generally split horizontally into thirds, with the sky as the top third, the water as the middle third, and the sand as the bottom third. The trees are placed off-center in the right vertical third of the piece.

You can also introduce thirds into your pieces using the focal elements rather than the background. In *Cardinal in the Oak*, 12" x 16" (30.5 x 40.6cm), the three tree branches serve to separate this image along thirds to create a balanced composition.

Rule 3—Add elements of interest in groupings of three or in odd rather than even numbers. When adding other layers of design elements to an art quilt, consider adding them in groupings of three or in odd numbers. Three seems to be the magic number, but five, seven, or nine will also work. Studies on how the brain processes visual information have found that when we see pairs of items, our brain visualizes them as pairs, but when we see odd groups of items, our brain first analyzes them as pairs and then adds the extra parts. In other words, an odd number of items makes our brains work slightly harder to process the image and will suggest to our brains that we are getting something extra.

Rule 4—Place your design's focal point (the point of interest) to one side, not in the middle. In addition to not placing your focal point dead center (or too close to the edge) of your art quilt, you may want to consider placing your focal point at one of the four intersecting points of the nine-patch grid used to visualize the rule of thirds. This will create a more pleasing and interesting composition than if you placed your focal point at the center or very edge of the piece of art.

Rule 5—Nature doesn't have perfectly straight lines. Add many elements that are curved to your art quilts to avoid unnatural rigidly straight lines. Before adding strips of fabric as background pieces, first fussy cut the top of the strips so they have uneven or curved edges.

The odd number of evergreens adds visual interest to *Winter Morning*, 8" x 10" (20.3 x 25.4cm).

The rooster's legs in *Rise and Shine!*, 16" x 20" (40.6 x 50.8cm), sit in a dip toward the left of the ground cover rather than being centered. Notice how the main body of the rooster aligns generally with the left third line of the nine-patch grid.

In this close-up of *Miss Dragonfly*, you can see the many curved lines I included in the grasses and the body and wings of the dragonfly.

When cutting elements like background grasses and strips of vegetation, add sharper spikes and rolling edges rather than flat tips.

Rule 6—Do not position objects too close to the edges, as they may be cut off. Too much work goes into adding beautiful elements to an art quilt to have them end up trimmed off or covered by a matting or binding.

I lost some of the tree details on the left and bottom edges of this autumn panel because I wasn't thinking about losing ⅛" (3.2mm) to ¼" (6.4mm) when trimming or adding bindings.

I kept my trimming line in mind as I placed the lake grasses on the bottom edge of this *Over the Cattails* art quilt.

Rule 7—Include a piece of black in your design to make the other elements shine brighter. You might have to try it to believe it, but a bit of black can brighten a scene rather than darken it too much.

The black background of *October Twist*, 18" x 18" (45.7 x 45.7cm), contributes to the vibrancy of the yellows and oranges.

The black cityscape and dark gray oil derrick pump in *Deep in the Heart of Texas*, 12" x 16" (30.5 x 40.6cm), add interest to the piece by contrasting with the bright natural colors used for the animals and landscape.

Rule 8—Leave negative space in your design. Negative space is the empty space surrounding the main subjects of a piece. Don't make your design too busy. More is not always better.

The open snowy areas (negative spaces) in this piece help create an impression of the silence and peacefulness in a winter forest.

Rule 9—Take a black-and-white photo of your design. To help guide your choices with design elements and fabric selections, take a black-and-white photograph of the elements, whether those are fabrics, sketches, or inspiring images. For example, as you audition your fabrics, take a picture of them together, and edit the photo to be black and white. You'll be able to see if your fabric choices are too light or too dark for a scene.

In this art quilt, *The Old Pine Tree*, 24" x 36" (61 x 91.4cm), the black-and-white photo clearly shows that the green fabrics behind the old pine are a bit too dark—the beautiful pine boughs get lost atop the background. Had I looked at a black-and-white photo of these fabrics during selection, I would have realized I needed to use lighter green fabrics for the background.

Rule 10—Do not always follow the rules. If you rely on design rules too often, your work may become formulaic and predictable. I have heard it said, however, that you should be able to support your choice to break the rules.

Breaking the rule that says to add elements of interest in odd numbers by including four trees in *Four Trees*, 18" x 18" (45.7 x 45.7cm), adds a serene quality and frames the heron.

Rather than placing the sailboat in *Sailing at Sunset* on an intersection of the nine-patch grid, placing it so far to the right accentuates the distance from land and feels more natural.

Audition and Choose Fabrics

I cannot stress enough the importance of choosing fabrics when making an art quilt. As you audition fabrics for use in any traditional quilt or art quilt, it takes practice to pick the best choices. Asking for advice from staff in a quilt shop or from another quilter can be helpful, and you will become more familiar with the fabrics and learn how best to use them as you practice. Try grouping your fabrics to see if the colors and patterns will work together or if one or more just does not fit. You can even practice matching fabric colors against completed quilts or art quilts.

I have dedicated the next few pages to fabric selection. As you choose fabrics for your art quilts, consider the following:

- types of fabric—use mostly tightly woven cottons that will result in a minimum of edge-fraying
- fabric texture—choose, based on your subject, whether to use all the same smooth texture or mix textures for added interest
- fabric color—try matching cool or warm colors and maybe add some lighter tints and darker shades
- fabric pattern—use a wide variety of fabric patterns that will complement the subject

Types of Fabric

Cottons are my fabrics of choice for art quilts. Cottons are easier to work with and less slippery than some other fabrics. Within the cotton category, flannels tend to have a large weave that fray the most, quilting cottons have a plain weave and a lot of body, and batiks have a tight weave that will fray the least in the process of raw-edge

Here are some examples of quilting cottons, from the tightest weaves (batiks with minimal fraying) to the largest weaves (flannels with lots of fraying).

To match a green to the grape patterned fabric, I placed green fabric options next to it. The green in the middle is the best match because it has matching yellow tones.

To match a blue to the grape-patterned fabric, I placed blue fabric options next to it. The lightest blue has too much white in it and the middle blue has too much of an aqua color, but the other three might work.

TIP

One of the most important fabric choices for an art quilt is choosing the color for the art canvas or border—the right color, often something that contrasts with the main image, will put the scene or subject in the spotlight.

collage quilting—almost like working with paper. If I could find every fabric in a batik, I would use batiks almost exclusively. However, when I see the perfect color (hue), value (lightness or darkness), or a desirable design, print, or pattern in a piece of fabric, even if it isn't a batik, I'll use it. If you take the time to spray your fabrics with spray sizing before using them, they will fray less.

Fabric Texture

Most often my cotton fabrics have a smooth texture. At times, an art quilt calls me to use something with a different texture, like gold lamé fabric for a sun, a linen for texture in a beach, sparkly tulle for some shine on the water, wool for a fluffy sheep, a bit of interesting trim, or other embellishments to create desired effects. These special fabrics and woven cottons, like linens and flannels, fray more than traditional quilting cottons and the edges of shiny fabrics and trims pose an array of problems. Keep this in mind if you don't want to battle fraying edges.

Fabric Color

In a picture, painting, or art quilt, the mood is the atmosphere or feeling expressed. Colors (and patterns) can create certain moods and feelings in art, so it is important to understand the psychological effects colors might have and to use that information to strengthen your art. Ask yourself what mood you're trying to convey and what colors and tones you might need to fit this mood.

Do you want the art quilt to be tranquil? Using sweet pastel colors, soothing cool blues and greens, or happy

Mix in fabrics with different textures, like this cork and these linens, to create added interest.

Flannel and wool fabrics offer great tactile and visual texture and can build depth in an art quilt.

I used calming shades of blue to create a peaceful mood in this art quilt from the *Touch of Teal* series.

Las Vegas, 16" x 20" (40.6 x 50.8cm), is a colorful piece, but the colors are muted and include darker blues and grays to help create a more subdued mood.

COLOR AND MOOD

Red
can stimulate and increase energy, sometimes literally increasing a person's heart rate, and it's a great color to make a dramatic statement. Since red has high visibility, use it in moderation to draw attention to certain design elements.

Orange
adds vibrancy and can make people feel energized and enthusiastic. Like red, it draws attention and shows movement, but it's not as overpowering. It is aggressive but balanced—a strong color that can also be inviting and friendly.

Yellow
increases happiness and lifts the spirits. Accents of energetic yellow can help the viewer to feel optimistic and cheerful. However, yellow tends to reflect a lot of light and can irritate viewers. Too much yellow will be overwhelming, so use it sparingly.

Green
can calm nerves, increase concentration, and make people feel optimistic, refreshed, and calm. It is the easiest color on the eyes and should be used to create balance in a design.

Blue
provides a calming effect and can make people feel safe and relaxed. Dark blues can create a sophisticated atmosphere, but using too much can create a cold, disengaged feeling. Light blues give a more relaxed, friendly feeling and can be used to create bright, calm atmospheres.

Purple
speaks of royalty, wealth, and mystery, and it combines the energy of red with the calm of blue. Use deeper purples to make a design look luxurious and decadent or lighter purples to convey sweet romance and mystery.

Pink
makes people feel playful and romantic and represents femininity, sensitivity, and tenderness. It's inherently sweet, cute, and charming.

Brown
makes people feel grounded and creates a sense of stability and support. It's warm, friendly, practical, and dependable, but brown can also be used to create dark, stagnant, or overly traditional moods, as well.

Gray
fills the space between black and white. Gray can be cool, elegant, and conservative but it can also be used to convey an air of mystery.

White
conveys purity, innocence, and simplicity. Using a lot of white color in a design creates a minimalist aesthetic and a fresh, clean look. It's also the most neutral of all the colors.

Black
feels sophisticated, classic, and serious. It conveys power, luxury, and elegance, but also professionalism, neutrality, and simplicity. Black is bold and mysterious but also evokes mourning and sadness.

The fabrics across the top row are warmer versions of blue, green, and red—they likely contain more yellow or gold dye. The fabrics across the bottom row are cooler versions of blue, green, and red—they likely contain more gray or silver dye. When matching fabrics, try to stick with one family or the other (warm or cool) so your fabrics will blend better.

colors, like bright and warm yellow, orange, and red, can uplift the mood of a piece.

Is the art intended to be dark and disturbing? Gray and black are the first colors that come to mind, but any dark and muted colors can convey a sad or solemn mood. Depending on how they are used, colors like blue, green, brown, and beige can create this atmosphere, as well.

I am mostly self-taught when it comes to color theory. Here are a few of my simple observations to consider while selecting fabric colors and hues. Cool colors include blue, green, and light purple. They tend to be calm and soothing. They remind us of water, sky, and even ice and snow. Warm colors are oranges, reds, and yellows; they can represent excitement and emotion. Think of sunlight and heat. Choose colors that work with the chosen mood or atmosphere you're trying to create with your art quilt. See Color and Mood on page 26 for more details.

If blue (cool) was added to a red fabric as it was dyed, the fabric will still be a warm color, but will read as just a little cooler. If yellow (warm) was added to the red fabric in the dyeing process, the red will read as just a little warmer. In auditioning reds for my project, I make my selections based on this—for example, I will match reds that all read cooler because they have a bluish tone, rather than mixing in reds with warmer yellow tones. Fabrics are also "tinted" with white to make lighter tints and "shaded" with blacks to make darker shades; bright, striking "pretty" colors will also need some dull or less striking "not-as-pretty" lights and darks to help them shine.

Fabric Pattern

As a rule, avoid using plain fabrics in art quilts. Plain colors and solids often appear flat, whereas patterned fabrics add movement and depth. A solid fabric will also tend to stand out excessively when placed next to patterned fabrics. Patterns can be used in the same way

This rainy sky would work well in an art quilt that requires a darker mood.

A bright sky pattern can uplift the overall mood of your art quilt.

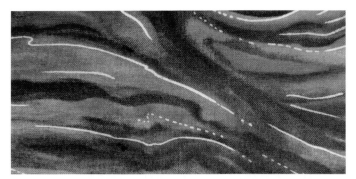

A swirling water pattern that includes a multitude of soothing colors can be used to create a tranquil composition or to convey happy movement.

A stormy curling water pattern can be used to add tension to a piece.

Landscape quilting prints can be applied to fabric in the traditional way, but they can also be digitally printed. The landscape quilting prints that are digitally printed on fabrics are very vibrant and have a very high print quality, but the weave can often have large threads and the prints don't soak through to the back of the fabric.

The printed fabrics on the left were designed specifically for art quilting. The fabrics on the right are traditional quilting fabrics that could be used to represent similar elements in an art quilt. You may already have some of these traditional quilting fabrics in your stash!

as color to convey mood in an art quilt. The following sky and water fabrics are examples of how powerful patterns can be for creating an atmosphere:

Patterns can either be printed onto fabric or applied using dye (either in a factory or by hand). Each has different benefits and drawbacks but both types can be used to enhance your art quilts.

Manufactured Printed Fabrics—Manufactured printed cotton fabrics (versus dyed fabrics) fall into two broad categories of prints—traditional quilting prints and landscape quilting prints. I use a mix of both.

When evaluating traditional quilting prints for use in art quilting, I try to choose a variety of patterns like crosshatches, minute florals, and "mottled" or "blender" fabrics. Often in art quilting you want the different colors of the fabrics to blend. One way you can achieve this is by adding mottled or blender fabrics to the designs. "Mottled" fabrics look hand-dyed and have graduating shades of color in irregular patterns. "Blender" fabrics have a tone-on-tone or washed appearance that help blend different components together.

Mottled fabrics have irregular, spotty patterns created with various shades of the same base color.

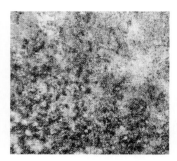

The tone-on-tone neutral wash appearance of "blender" fabrics helps surrounding fabrics flow together.

This landscape quilting print was digitally printed; it has sharp details and vibrant colors.

This is just one example of the many dyed patterns that can be found on batik fabrics. It would work very well in an art quilt.

Dyed Fabrics—Batiks are beautiful fabrics with factory-dyed colors and patterns, rather than printed. They are used in traditional quilting and in art quilting, and they come in an extensive spectrum of colors and values. Patterns dyed onto batiks can often enhance the mood and message of your art quilt. Also, rather than using these factory-dyed quilting fabrics, you may want to explore using some beautiful hand-dyed fabrics. Painting or adding color to fabrics already purchased is another technique to consider. See Using Temporary Marks and Adding Color to Fabrics on page 49.

Finding Fabrics

You might ask, "How much fabric do you need or should you have?" **MORE**. "How much should you buy of any one fabric?" You might want to start out with an eighth or quarter yard or a fat quarter. However, if you think the fabric might make a good background for a scene, a half yard would be a good idea. Retracing your steps to repurchase more of a piece of fabric is a science, requiring artful moves and dedication. "Where will you find the right fabric?" Your stash, your friends' stashes, local and other quilt shops, trade shows, and online. I always support my local quilt shop, but when I travel, I am always on the hunt for new quilt shops to "mine for gold." I also go to trade shows that feature vendors from many different parts of the world. If all else fails, I search online. It is helpful to know manufacturers, stock numbers, and design names, but you can often find what you're looking for by glancing through a search engine's image results or browsing direct-selling sites and fabric company websites.

BACKS OF FABRICS

Remember that the backs of fabrics will often be a different tint of the same hue or a lighter version of your pattern—you might prefer to use that side of the fabric in your project instead.

The back of this dark bark fabric, shown on the left, has a similar texture, but reverses the colors to create a lighter bark pattern.

The winter sky in this piece looks like it is composed of many different fabrics, but most of the strips are the front or back of the same gray-and-white dotted fabric.

I used the back sides of the background fabrics in this quilt, including the stone wall print, to create the impression of a misty morning.

Support your local quilt shops! *Abbi May's Fabric Shop in Muskegon, Michigan; Owner Linda Hazekamp*

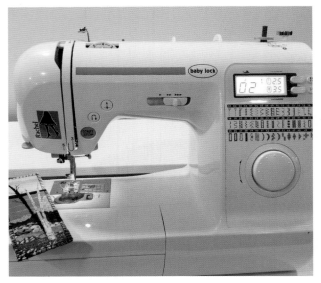
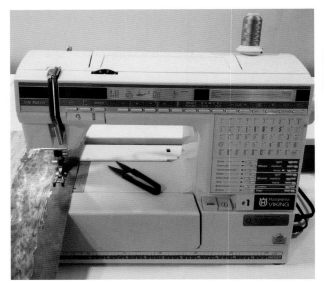

Chapter 3

My at-home sewing machine, the Viking Husqvarna 1, and my travel sewing machine, the Baby Lock Rachel, are both good examples of domestic sewing machines. Surprisingly, art quilting only requires the features of a basic sewing machine.

Tools and Materials

To turn the ideas from the Design Inspiration chapter into art quilts or to create the projects later in this book, you'll need a few standard tools and materials. You may have some of these tools already in your sewing stash, like a sewing machine and fabric, but you may need to purchase others, like art canvases or A2 cards.

DOMESTIC SEWING MACHINE

Generally, my sewing machines are set to a 2.5mm stitch width. I currently use a Viking Husqvarna 1 at home and a lighter Baby Lock Rachel for teaching on the road. Look for these features and helpful tools:

- open-toe foot
- free-motion foot (optional)
- sewing machine needles:
  ○ machine embroidery needles; 70/80
  ○ topstitch needles (optional)
- quilting gloves with rubber fingers (optional)

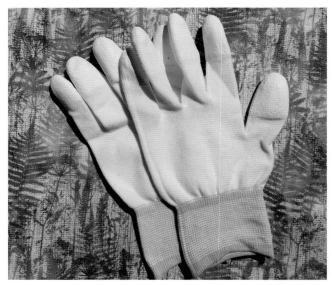

Quilting gloves are optional, but they can make stitching on art quilts much smoother and easier.

TIP

Puddle several inches of each thread atop your fabric piece to audition thread colors and choose the best match. Using a larger amount of thread will give you a better idea of how well the colors match than a single strand of thread will.

Along with the regular quilting fabrics used to create the decorative pieces on top of the art quilt (the green and tan fabrics above), you'll also need cotton backing fabric and quilt batting or fusible fleece.

THREADS

There are a few important things to look for when shopping for thread:
- pretty colors
- thread shades that don't overpower fabric choices
- polyester invisible thread (used occasionally for less visibility)
- bobbin threads:
  - neutral colors like light gray, white, tan, beige, or black
  - matching color to top thread (occasionally needed)

It's always a good practice for art quilting to have a wide range of available thread colors. They will be useful for matching fabrics and have the added benefit of looking like beautiful wall art when organized!

FABRICS

Along with the quilting fabrics discussed in the Audition and Choose Fabrics section on page 24, you'll need a few other types of fabric to complete your art quilts:
- cotton backing fabric
- quilt batting, thin (with quilt basting spray) or fusible fleece, such as Pellon® TP971F Fusible Thermolam® Plus or 987F Fusible Fleece
- printable fabric sheets for inkjet printers, such as June Tailor® Sew-In Colorfast Fabric Sheets™ for Ink Jet Printers

June Tailor Colorfast Fabric Sheets for Ink Jet Printers are easy to use in home printers and create quality fabric prints. I often work with them to create small, detailed art quilt pieces like the cardinals on these fabric art cards.

It can be easy to forget the differences between the different papers used for art quilting techniques, but here's a quick reminder:

Parchment paper or scrap paper from the back of a fusible web piece—This paper is not adhesive and won't stick to fabric. It can be used to protect your ironing surface and for combining small fabric pieces that already have adhesive applied to the back into larger units that can be peeled off the parchment paper and applied to the art quilt surface.

Freezer paper—The waxy side of this paper will temporarily stick to fabric. A drawing on freezer paper can be roughly cut out and pressed onto the front of fabric that already has adhesive applied to the back. You can fussy cut out the shape and then peel the freezer paper template from the fabric.

Fusible web—This is iron-on adhesive used solely for backing fabrics to add an adhesive layer. After the adhesive is pressed onto the fabric and has cooled, you peel the backing paper off to reveal the adhesive-covered fabric. The peeled-off scrap paper can be used for the same purposes as parchment paper.

IRON AND IRONING SUPPLIES

Start with what you have. Later consider the addition of a small iron (I like the Steamfast SF-717 Steam Iron). Also get your hands on the following tools:
- small ironing board or flannel-covered board— approximately 20" x 20" (50.8 x 50.8cm):
  - a small ironing board is good for traveling and to keep next to your sewing machine for quick ironing right as you add pieces to sew down
  - flannel-covered foam-core boards that you can both pin to and press on are useful for parchment collaging
- starch or starch alternatives, like Mary Ellen's Best Press™ spray
- freezer paper for making templates that will temporarily **stick** to fabric
- surface protector sheets that are **non-stick** and will protect surfaces while ironing:
  - parchment baking paper (not freezer paper)
  - scrap paper from the back of Pellon Wonder-Under® fusible web (I use this; it's free!)
  - Teflon™ sheet (these work well, but are smaller and more expensive)

ROTARY CUTTING SUPPLIES

Certain rotary cutting tools will make creating the curved edges required for natural art quilts much easier:
- rotary cutters—28mm recommended; 45mm and 60mm are supplemental
- self-healing mats such as Olfa® rotary mats, which are durable and easy on rotary cutters, in various sizes
- rotary cutting rulers measuring 2½" x 12½" (6.4 x 31.8cm) and 12½" x 12½" (31.8 x 31.8cm)

Placing a piece of parchment paper between your fabric and your iron will protect the fabric from possible heat damage or marks.

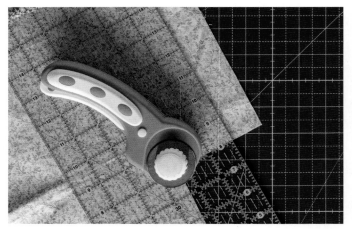

A rotary cutter, self-healing mat, and clear rulers and grids are all useful tools to own for sewing and quilting in general, but are indispensable to creating the rolling hills and waves, natural curving tree trunks, and other natural elements featured in landscape art quilts.

Designate different scissors for different uses. Smaller pairs will be useful for fussy cutting detail pieces, and some scissors will work best for fabric while others are best for use with paper.

Quality colored pencils, erasable or iron-away marking pens, and ceramic chalk pencils will help you temporarily mark the shapes you need to cut without permanently damaging your fabric.

You'll want to use a large glue stick because a small one takes too long, PVA craft glue like Aleene's Original Tacky Glue because it is more permanent, and temporary basting glue like Roxanne Glue-Baste-It with a thin tip that will deliver fine lines of glue.

A2 cards and envelopes are an approachable and useful size to work with, but you can try other sizes if you'd like to make larger or smaller cards for your friends and family.

You can cleanly and easily finish your art quilts of all sizes by mounting them on plain standard stretched canvases.

SCISSORS AND SUCH

In art quilting, using the right pair of scissors or accessories for the right job can make a huge difference for creating sharp edges and working with small pieces. You should keep the following readily available:

- small curved fabric scissors, such as Karen Kay Buckley's 3¾" Perfect Curved Scissors™
- larger fabric scissors, such as Karen Kay Buckley's 6" Perfect Scissors
- paper scissors
- tweezers

MARKING PENS/PENCILS

These tools will help with temporarily but clearly marking your fabric:

- iron-away pen, such as the Pilot FriXion® Ball Erasable Gel Pen
- chalk pencil, such as the Sewline™ Fabric Pencil with white ceramic lead
- colored pencils, such as Derwent Inktense Colored Pencils

ADHESIVES

Along with the adhesive tools like batting and basting spray or fusible web that are listed with the fabrics, you'll also need:

- large glue stick, such as Elmer's® Craft BOND® Extra Strength
- PVA (polyvinyl acetate) craft glue, such as Aleene's® Original Tacky Glue®
- temporary basting glue, such as Roxanne Glue-Baste-It®

BLANK CARDS FOR FABRIC ART CARD PROJECTS

You can use any size of cardstock to create fabric art card projects, but for the projects in this book, you'll need:

- A2 cards—4¼" x 5½" (42 x 59.4cm) cardstock with envelopes

STRETCHED ART CANVASES FOR MOUNTED PROJECTS

The Standard Canvas Sizes chart on page 17 should give you an idea of your options for mounting art quilts of various sizes, but there is one average size that will always be useful:

- 8" x 10" x ½" depth (20.3 x 25.4 x 1.5cm depth)

Chapter 4

Bring Your Art Quilt to Life: The Construction Process

At this point, you have a design in mind, you have reference photos and sketches, and you've chosen the medium, size, and orientation of the project, as well as the color scheme and fabrics. You've perhaps adjusted your plan based on the design rules and guidelines and assembled the tools you'll need. Now it's time to begin physical construction of your art quilt.

Start building the quilt sandwich with backing and batting or fusible fleece.

Step 1: Start Making the Quilt Sandwich

A quilt sandwich comprises the cotton quilt backing, the fuzzy quilt batting, and the finished quilt top. As a starting point for creating your quilt sandwich, adhere the backing and batting together. There are two workable types of batting to use. The easiest to use is fusible fleece, which can easily be ironed to the cotton backing. The second is cotton batting, which is adhered to cotton backing with quilt basting spray. Cut your cotton backing and batting or fusible fleece pieces approximately ¼" (6.4mm) larger than your desired finished size to allow for shrinkage during ironing. Retrim after ironing.

If I am going to be making the starts of several quilt sandwiches, I usually adhere large pieces of cotton backing and batting together ahead of time, then cut these larger bases into smaller premade sets.

If you are going to mount your art quilt on a fabric-covered stretched canvas frame, in most cases your quilt sandwich will need to be about 1"–3" (2.5–7.6cm) smaller in width and height than the canvas; for example, a 14" x 18" (35.6 x 45.7cm) quilt sandwich for a 16" x 20" (40.6 x 50.8cm) finished product. You will want to plan early for this smaller quilt sandwich to achieve that 1"–3" (2.5–7.6cm) border surrounding and accentuating your art quilt.

Step 2: Back Fabric with Fusible Web

There are several different types of adhesives that can be used on the backs of fabrics to keep them in place as you stitch them down onto an art quilt. Fusible web is a manufactured fiber that will melt in mere seconds when heated. One side is paper-backed and ironable onto the back of a porous surface like fabric. Once the backed fabric is cool, the paper backing can be removed, and the fabric is ready to apply to your art quilt. I prefer the highly versatile Pellon 805 Wonder-Under. Fabrics backed by Wonder-Under remain soft and easily sewn and unlike other fusible webs I've used, no gooey substance will stick to your sewing machine needle.

You can easily back fabric pieces measuring just a few inches or centimeters, a whole group of fabrics strips cut the width of your project, or even a fat quarter or entire yard.

If you want to back just enough fabric for one project, decide on the width of the project. Let's say you chose a 9" x 7" (22.9 x 17.8cm) art quilt. All fabric strips for the art quilt can be cut to 9" (22.9cm) wide. Decide on an approximate height for each strip by looking at your sketch, adding up to 1" (2.5cm) so that the strips aren't too short; for example, a 9" x 3" (22.9 x 7.6cm) strip should be cut to 9" x 3½–4" (22.9 x 8.9–10.2cm). Once you've cut these strips, you can back them all at once.

Backing fabrics with a product like Pellon 805 Wonder-Under paper-backed fusible web can streamline some parts of the art quilt process.

It's easy to back small pieces of fabric with fusible web using an iron.

> **TIP**
>
> Taking the time to spray your fabric with spray sizing or starch before applying fusible web will stiffen the fabric and reduce fraying.

Backing the fabric is simple. Place parchment paper on your ironing surface and then place your piece of fabric face down atop the parchment paper. Next, place your fusible web fiber side down and smooth side up on top of the fabric. With the iron on a very high heat setting, press for about five seconds, making sure to cover all the edges. Trim away any paper edges that stick off the edges of the fabric using a rotary cutter or scissors, then allow the adhered set to cool for five minutes to an hour. Once everything is cool, remove the paper backing by wrinkling up the set a bit and peeling from the edge. If you notice the web still adhering to the paper rather than the fabric, repress.

Backing all your strips at once is a great way to save some time.

> **TIP**
>
> Your iron will invariably pick up stray bits of adhesive. Wipe your hot iron as soon as possible with a used dryer sheet (free!) or a melamine sponge like Mr. Clean® Magic Eraser to remove the residue.

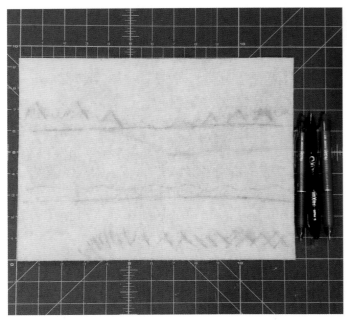

Use iron-away pens to roughly sketch the elements you want to include in your finished art quilt directly onto the front of the batting.

As you create your art quilt, you'll work from the top down, filling in your sketch with your fabric pieces and erasing the lines as you iron.

Step 3: Sketch Your Design onto the Batting

You can use an erasable marker, like a Pilot FriXion Ball iron-away pen, to sketch the major sections of the composition onto the front of your quilt sandwich's fuzzy batting. If you don't like the balance of your original sketch, you can iron it away and start again. When you are pleased with your sketch, you may want to go over the sketched lines lightly with a lead pencil. As you work from top to bottom building your scene, the ironing will erase the original lines and they will be lost. Don't worry about light pencil lines showing through because the fabric will cover them easily. Also, these lines are just a guide. The improvisational nature of art quilting means you may need to change your plans as you work.

Step 4: Cut and Add Background

Set the combined backing and batting of the quilt sandwich set atop your ironing surface with the batting side up and prepare to add the background pieces. The background of an art quilt can be very simple like the two-piece backgrounds I often use as backdrops for flower arrangements, or it can have several strips or pieces like the more complicated backgrounds I create for landscape scenes.

You can create a simple background using just one or two pieces of fabric. I often use simple backgrounds for floral arrangements.

A background can also consist of many layered strips, some cut simply, some fussy cut to imitate realistic landscape elements.

You will need to collage (arrange) the background strips from top to bottom, each overlapping the previous strip until you have covered the batting from top to bottom. For example, the background in the photo above was built by first pressing the sky strip across the top edge of the batting, then layering the rest of the strips on top in the order in which they appear in the quilt: clouds, bushes, the hill on the left, the vegetation on the right, the water, the left sand layers, the final sand layer, and the grasses in front. While layering your fabric pieces, you can really evaluate how well your chosen fabrics are working together. You can use a black-and-white photo of the fabric arrangement for a different perspective on how the fabrics are blending. I like to say that the fabrics will tell you when the colors or element placement in the art quilt feels right. It is like watching magic happen in front of your eyes.

Make any needed adjustments and once you are happy with the arrangement of the layers, press. **Note:** When collaging together pieces of an art quilt, before pressing an entire section down, think ahead to determine if any pieces or elements still need to be placed under the edge of any of the strips. If so, press the center of the sections in place, and leave the edges unpressed so you can add more pieces under the edges.

Here's an example of different unassembled (left) and assembled (right) background fabric strip options for art quilts of similar scenes. The art quilt on the right is a finished piece with the foreground details added and stitched down. These are just 3" x 5" (7.6 x 12.7cm). You can pack a lot of detail into the background!

Step 5: Stitch Down Background Layer

The pattern printed on each piece of fabric should guide you in choosing how to stitch it down and the pattern and color of the fabric should guide you in choosing your thread colors. Stitch across each strip as closely to the top edge as you possibly can. Then, for several rows through the middle of each strip, you might stitch in rounded cloud-like meanders through a sky, loose waves over a hillside, tight waves on a sandy beach, spiked points for grass, or other natural shapes inspired by the scene you're trying to create. You should ensure that all the background strips are stitched down before you begin to add a second layer of elements like trees or plants. You can see how difficult it would have been to stitch across the summer scene background strips in the art quilt below with the trees in the way. Ask me how I know! Thread color and topstitch examples for this summer scene are:

Here is an example of what a background with multiple strips might look like stitched down. I stitch down the edge of each strip with matching thread and then add stitched lines to both hold the pieces together and add to the natural feel of the elements. You can see the smooth lines that give the impression of flowing water, the rocky lines meandering through the sandy stone hill, the jagged spikes in the grasses and vegetation, and other natural shapes created by the stitching.

Light blue stitching in wavy cloud shapes across the sky

Medium tan across the top and in waves across the left hill

Medium blue or shiny opalescent across the top and in two or three more wavy rows through the blue waves

Light tan in dune-like swirls across the top and through the sand-colored strip

Olive green around the edges of the pines and up the middle of the trees in pine-like spikes

Medium tan or olive green in grass-like spikes up and down the right brownish green grass clump

Grass green in grass-like spikes across grassy strip in the bottom right corner

This is *Four Seasons Summer Breezes*, 8" x 10" (20.3 x 25.4cm), the finished art quilt created using the background strips shown at the top of page 37. The background layer is stitched down before the second layer of trees is added. Imagine trying to stitch the background pieces with the top elements (the trees) already in place. It just wouldn't work.

Step 6: Fussy Cut and Add Other Design Elements

It's fussy cutting time! In the example summer scene below, the second layer is the tree trunk layer (the tree leaves are an additional layer on top of this). I rotary cut thin tree slivers from birch patterned, black, and even brown fabric. Notice that I have used the artist's technique of including black (tree trunks) in my scene to create a sense of depth and allow the other colors in the piece to shine brighter.

You might want to take the time here to fussy cut elements that will be applied to the third layer, like leaves or other smaller elements, but set these aside until after you've stitched down the second layer.

Now press the fussy-cut second layer elements atop the stitched-down background layer. If you are adding strips of trees, iron them on so that there are natural curves in the trunks and branches. Begin ironing the tree trunks onto the background from the bottom, moving toward the top of the quilt. This will allow you to bend them as you iron.

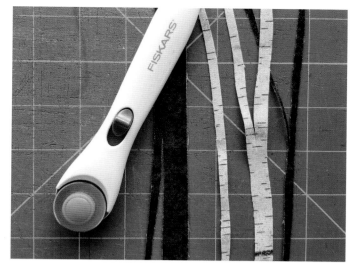

Here are rotary-cut tree trunks, ready to be artfully arranged onto the background.

Here are a few other types of fussy cut plants and trees that can be fun to add to nature scenes.

This photo shows the second layer of tree trunks already pressed down and sewn to the background with the third layer of leaves pressed down on top. Notice how the tree trunks in this second layer also overlap one another. Choose your arrangement and press them on in that order to create layers within your individual layers.

One of the easiest ways to create many natural fussy-cut leaf details at once is to cut one long, thin strip of fabric and then cut small oval shapes from the strip.

Step 7: Stitch Down Each Added Layer

Stitch down the elements of the second layer. If you are going to be stitching trees, consider drawing on secondary branches with an iron-away pen. This is helpful when teaching yourself how to add more branches. For the trees in this illustration, I stitched up one side of each tree trunk and down the other, "thread painting" secondary tree branches here and there. I also stitched wavering bark lines up the centers of the wider trees.

After the second layer is stitched down, press on the third layer (in the example summer scene, the third layer includes tree leaves only). I often add a third layer of low plants and stitch them in place. Small elements such as leaves need to be pressed firmly in place, but don't necessarily need to be stitched down. Once each layer of your quilt top is pressed on and stitched (if necessary), your combined backing, batting, and finished quilt top form your completed quilt sandwich.

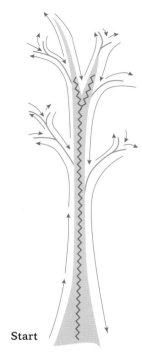

In this art quilt, the second layer of tree trunks is stitched down. The third layer of leaves only needed to be pressed down.

This diagram shows the process I follow when stitching down tree trunks and adding thread "branches" to the finished piece. First, I stitch up the left edge of the trunk, taking time to follow the outside of each branch and stitch extra branches, following that edge up around the top of the tree and down the right edge. Next, I stitch vertical rows in the center of the trunk to give the impression of bark's texture.

Start

In this view of the back of a quilt, you can more clearly see the stitching used for each piece and layer.

Here's another close-up example of adding additional plants and final layer stitching, this one from *Reaching Upward, Panel #2*, 28" x 36" (72 x 96cm). The tree trunk was pressed and stitched onto the background as the second layer, then the pine boughs and grass patch at the bottom of the trunk were added as a third layer.

Step 8: Finish Your Art Quilt

Method One: Raw Edges—Press the art quilt top with moisture (either use steam or spray the surface with water, starch, or starch alternative). Square up the sides of the art quilt with a ruler and rotary cutter. If desired, glue the art quilt to a fabric-covered art canvas with PVA craft glue. See Covering a Stretched Art Canvas on page 44.

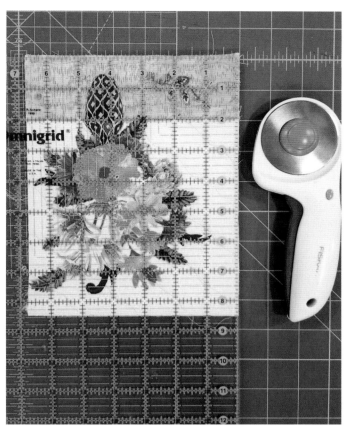

I finished *Summer Breezes* with raw edges—a viable option that requires minimal work. I then mounted it on a fabric-covered stretched canvas.

After ironing the art quilt with moisture, square up the edges. Using a clear ruler will allow you to align your quilt properly before trimming.

Winter Ice, 8" x 10" (20.3 x 25.4cm), demonstrates how a raw-edged art quilt mounted on a covered art canvas can still have a clean, finished appearance.

Method Two: Adding a Binding—Press the art quilt top with moisture. Square up the sides of the art quilt with a ruler and rotary cutter. Cut a ⅞" (2.2cm) wide binding strip (cut multiple strips, if necessary) the length of the distance around the edges of the art quilt, plus a couple of inches for good measure. For example, a 9" x 7" (22.9 x 17.8cm) quilt would need a strip that is 32+" (81.3+cm) long: the two 9" (22.9cm) sides = 18" (45.7cm), the two 7" (17.8cm) sides = 14" (35.6cm), and together all four sides = 32" (81.3cm). Back any fabric binding strips with your favorite fusible web.

Sew the binding to the front of the art quilt with a ¼" (6.4mm) seam, beginning at the lower left corner of the quilt to make the join least visible. Press the binding flat on the front, then roll it over around the edge of the quilt sandwich and press it flat to the back. If desired, glue the art quilt to a fabric-covered art canvas with PVA craft glue. See Covering a Stretched Art Canvas on page 44.

This quilt in the *Over the Cattails* series features a bound edge.

Here is a binding strip, cut to the correct ⅞" (2.2cm) width and the length needed based on the dimensions of the art quilt top. It's also backed with fusible web and is ready for the binding process.

If you want to live on the wild and crazy side, you can cut your border strips from fabrics featuring the colors or patterns found on the edges of the quilt. As you sew on the binding, cut and restart sewing every time the color on the edge of the quilt changes. This art quilt, *The Big Bend*, 18" x 24" (45.7 x 61cm), features a multicolored binding created using seven different fabric strips. It's also mounted on a fabric-covered art canvas.

Method Three: Set into a Border—Press the art quilt top with moisture. Square up the sides of the art quilt with a ruler and rotary cutter. Cut a 3½" (8.9cm) wide border strip (cut multiple strips, if necessary) the length of the distance around the edges of the art quilt, plus 12" (30.5cm) to allow for the corners. For example, a 9" x 7" (22.9 x 17.8cm) quilt would need a strip that is 44" (1.1m) long: the two 9" (22.9cm) sides = 18" (45.7cm), the two 7" (17.8cm) sides = 14" (35.6cm), together all four sides = 32" (81.3cm), and adding 12" (30.5cm) = 44" (1.1m).

Cut the long strip(s) into four smaller strips, two the height of the quilt (7" [17.8cm] in the example quilt) plus 3" (7.6cm) and two the width of the quilt (9" [22.9cm] in the example quilt) plus 3". For example, you would end up with two 10" (25.4cm) long strips and two 12" (30.5cm) long strips for the example 9" x 7" (22.9 x 17.8cm) quilt.

Using a ¼" (6.4cm) seam allowance, sew the border strips cut to the height of the art quilt plus 3" (7.6cm) onto the left and right edges of the art quilt. Press the seams toward the border and trim square. Then add the border strips cut to the width of the art quilt plus 3" (7.6cm) to the top and bottom edges, press the seams, and trim square.

After I set my art quilts into borders, I often mount them on stretched art canvases. If you plan to mount your art quilt with attached border to a canvas, adjust the length and width of the border strips based on the size of your art canvas. To calculate the width needed for the border strips, place your art quilt in the center of the canvas and measure the distance between the edges of the art quilt and the edges of the canvas, then add 1¾" (4.4cm). This will allow enough fabric to create a ¼" (6.4mm) seam when you sew the border strips to your art quilt and enough fabric to wrap around the edges of the art canvas. For example, if there is 3" (7.6cm) between the edge of your art quilt and the edge of your canvas, you should cut 4¾" (12.1cm) border strips.

When mounting a bordered art quilt to a canvas, square up the edges of the borders and press. Using a large glue stick, add glue to the edges of the back side of the borders. Center the front side of the art quilt on top of the canvas and carefully flip the whole thing over to work on the back side. Wrap and stretch the borders around the back edges of the canvas. (Recheck the front side and make any adjustments needed to correctly center the art quilt design.) Fold and glue the borders down to the back side of the canvas frame. See Covering a Stretched Art Canvas on page 44.

Both of these art quilts from the Birches in Blue and Green series are set in borders and then mounted on art canvases.

A 3½" (8.9cm) strip of fabric can be used to create a 3" border to nicely frame your art quilt.

Audition many different fabrics to find the perfect fabric to highlight your art quilt. This fabric can be used alone to cover a stretched canvas for mounting or can be sewn directly to the art quilt as a thin binding or a thick border.

Mounting Method 1: Covering a Stretched Art Canvas—
To finish a project by mounting it on a canvas, you'll
need a stretched art canvas, a large glue stick, and fabric.
Choose a color of fabric that will complement and frame
the colors in your art quilt. After I complete an art quilt,
I spend a lot of time auditioning fabrics to cover the art
canvas. It's one of the most difficult fabric choices I make.
Like a wooden frame around a photograph or painting,
the fabrics frame the art quilt.

For ½" (1.5cm) deep stretched art canvas frames,
cut fabric 2½" (3.8cm) larger than the dimensions of the
canvas frame. For example, for an 8" x 10" (20.3 x 25.4cm)
stretched canvas, cut the fabric to 10½" x 12½"
(26.7 x 31.8cm).

1. Using a large glue stick, with the fabric **face down**,
apply glue liberally in a 1"–2" (2.5–5.1cm) swath around
all four outside edges on the back of the fabric. Place the
art canvas face down in the center of the fabric with the
wet glue applied. Work quickly as the glue is fast drying.

2. Fold the longest edges over two parallel sides of the
frame and pull it taut.

3. On one of the short ends, fold in the end fabric, then
make a perpendicular line across the edge of the frame.
This will leave you with four diagonal tabs that need glue
applied to the inside surfaces. After applying glue to the
four tabs, fold these tabs over the short edge of the frame.

4. Repeat Step 3 on the opposite short end.

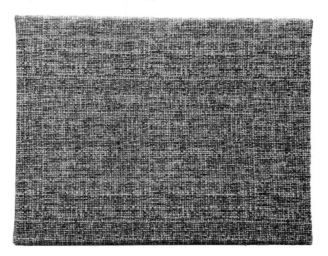

The finished wrapped canvas. Gluing your finished art quilt,
whether with raw edges or a sewn binding, onto a smooth
wrapped canvas is the quickest way to create a stunning
piece of easy-to-hang wall art.

Mounting Method 2: Hanging Sleeve for Mounting—If you want to finish your art quilt with a binding and don't want to mount it on a covered canvas, you can still create a hanging art quilt. Add a narrow sleeve to the top back of your quilt before stitching on the binding and you'll be able to slide a hanging rod or slat into the sleeve. You can also sew a sleeve to the bottom back of the quilt and insert a shorter rod or slat as weight to keep the quilt hanging straight.

Here are some basic directions. Use a flexible cotton in any color. Measure across the top edge of your quilt (where the sleeve will go) and subtract an inch or a few centimeters to determine the width of the sleeve. For the width of the sleeve, depending on the size of the quilt and the size of the hanging rod, you will want your sleeve to be 2"–3" (5.1–7.6cm) wide. For a 3" sleeve, the width of the starting fabric piece should be 6½" (16.5cm). This is double the finished sleeve width plus ½" (1.3cm) extra for each ¼" (6.2mm) seam. For example, to create a 3" (7.6cm) sleeve for a quilt that is 24" (61cm) wide, cut a starting fabric strip that is 23" (58.4cm) long and 6½" (16.5cm) wide.

Fold this fabric strip in half with the wrong sides together (like a hot dog bun) and press. Stitch a ¼" seam along each short edge, then turn right-side out. Press. Zigzag stitch the long raw-edged sides together. Pin the sleeve to the back of the quilt along the top edge, centering the sleeve so that you can't see the side edges beyond the edges of the quilt. Machine sew a basting stitch across the top of the quilt, about ⅛" from the edge, adhering the sleeve to the back of the quilt. Pin the bottom of the sleeve to the back of the quilt, allowing for a little slack so the quilt will hang better on a rod or slat. Without allowing for this slack on the back, you may have a bulge on the front of the quilt where the hanging rod goes through. Hand stitch across the bottom edge of this sleeve. Your stitches should only go through the backing and the batting. You should not see them on the front of the quilt. Now the quilt is ready for the binding to be added, and the top edge of the sleeve will be hidden under the binding.

TIP

Use a wooden dowel or curtain rod in your hanging top sleeve. For the bottom straightening sleeve, an old yardstick or piece of wooden slat from a lumber department will do the trick.

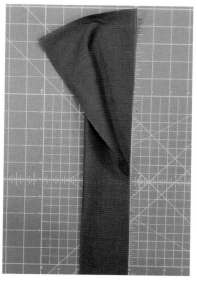

The back of this art quilt features both a hanging sleeve at the top and a straightening sleeve at the bottom. Notice the longer black, wooden hanging dowel on the top. The wooden slat in the bottom sleeve is shorter and would not normally be visible, but I pulled it out slightly for the photo.

This hanging sleeve fabric is folded right sides together to prepare for stitching the side ends shut.

TIP

Once your art quilts are finished, what's next? Of course, you can hang an art quilt or display it on an easel, but you can also use them as functional fabric pieces to create home decorations and accessories!

Skip the mounting steps and you can use your art quilt to create home décor items like throw pillows.

Art quilt designs can be sewn to tote bags or clothing, as well.

Chapter 5

Tips, Tricks, and Troubleshooting

As with any art form, sometimes things will not go as planned. The following techniques will help with some of the trickier parts of the art quilt process and provide you with skills you can use to solve any problems you might encounter or just add a unique creative flair to your own designs.

Fussy Cutting Techniques

Pictures are worth a thousand words. Grab your 28mm rotary cutter and a very sharp pair of small scissors and get ready!

Trees—You can use fabric with printed bark patterns, or you can use fabrics with just the hint of a pattern for trees. You can even add a bit of marker color or ink to plainer fabrics to add more dimension or specific tree bark spots or knots.

Tree Leaves—You can use fabrics patterned with specific leaf shapes or traditional fabrics that have interesting patterns.

Green Plants and Vegetation—You can use fabrics patterned with specific plant shapes or traditional fabrics that have interesting patterns.

Flowers—You can use fabrics patterned with specific flower shapes or traditional fabrics that have interesting patterns.

Ground Cover—You can use fabrics patterned with specific plant-like shapes or traditional fabrics that have interesting patterns. Patterned batiks are often very useful for creating general ground cover.

It's easy to cut thin strips of fabric with a rotary cutter. These are great to use for tree trunks and branches like those in this art quilt.

This cotton landscape fabric includes right side up and upside-down trees blended together. I focus on and cut out individual tree "blobs" to mimic realistic evergreens.

Cutting a narrow strip and then fussy cutting individual leaves from it is easier than trying to cut tiny leaves from a larger piece of fabric. I organize my precut leaves by color and size into small zippered plastic bags.

You can create fussy-cut plants in many different shapes, sizes, and colors to mimic the variety of plants that can be found in nature.

When fussy cutting seedy grasses or other long, thin stems and vines, I tend to leave a bit of extra space around the edges of the plant.

The impression of ground cover and general vegetation is best achieved by creating a mix of fussy-cut fabrics printed with organic or plant-like patterns and colors.

Stitching or Thread Painting Organically

I organically and intuitively stitch down my fabric pieces based on the pattern printed on each piece and the part of the landscape the piece is meant to convey. Sometimes this is as general as stitching jagged or flowing lines to convey grass or water textures, but in some cases, this can be more like thread painting.

Trees—Trees will usually involve stitching around the outside edge of the tree and creating a few not-perfectly straight bark lines in the tree trunks. Stitching can be used to add thin branch details, as well.

This view of the back of a *Three Pine Trees* art quilt demonstrates how conveying tree shapes is often more like thread painting than simple wavy line stitching.

These two photos show the front and back of some batik fabric cut into the shape of a stand of evergreens. I almost thread painted tree shapes into the fabric, adding tree trunk and branch patterns. Because of the matching thread, the texture from the stitching is subtle from the front, but clear if you look at the back.

Backgrounds—Stitching on backgrounds often involves highlighting specific parts of the background fabric's pattern or creating natural elements with thread.

Outlining Elements—One easy way to highlight pieces or details in your art quilts is to outline them by stitching around the outside edge.

This close-up on the main subject of the quilt shows how the combination of the pattern and the organic stitching conveys the hint of a slightly blurred leafy background behind the cardinal.

I created these small art quilts in the *Evergreen Ice* series because the backs of the sewn arrangements looked so pretty. I decided to mount some of these to really highlight the unusual beauty of the stitching.

Using Temporary Marks and Adding Color to Fabrics

Pens, pencils, inks, and fabric markers are all extremely useful during the process. They can be used as practical tools in planning your designs, marking fabric for cutting, or fixing small gaps between background strips, but they can also allow you the flexibility to get truly creative and add unique touches and details to your art quilts.

Iron-Away Pen—Test many erasable and iron-away pens to find the ones you like best. Some erasable pens have ink that disappears after a time or have tips that draw in a fat line. I haven't found any I like better than Pilot FriXion Ball pens. These pens were not created for use on fabric and the lines that are erased by heat will reappear in freezing temperatures, but this has never been a problem for me. No matter the brand of pen you choose to use, you should buy several different colors that will be clearly visible on lighter or darker fabrics.

Chalk Pencil—If you have to make temporary guide marks on dark fabrics, white works the best. I like the Sewline Fabric Pencil with white ceramic lead because the lead is superfine and always sharp. You can dampen the marking line to remove the white ceramic chalk.

I use iron-away pens to sketch my cutting lines onto my fabrics to test out how the finished piece might look and to ensure that I cut out the correct shape.

Use your iron-away pens on the backs of patterned fabrics to clearly outline areas and shapes you'd like to cut out.

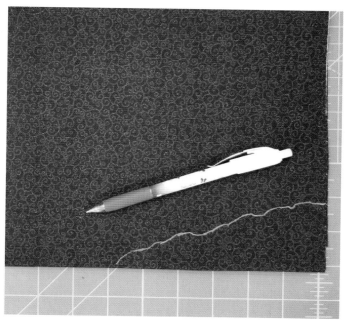

You can really see your cutting lines on dark pieces of fabric when you mark them with a white chalk pencil.

Colored Pencils and Markers—I first tried adding color to white birch trees that needed a few more black spots to stand out against the background. A regular permanent black marker did the trick. Colored pencils work for adding spot colors, as well. I use Derwent Inktense Colored Pencils, but any quality set of at least a dozen different colors will help add variety to your art quilts.

Every so often two thin, overlapping pieces of fabric may split apart during stitching. Rather than patching the hole with fabric and restitching, you can hide small gaps with markers or colored pencils.

Once I realized the blending possibilities of colored pencils, I was in love. As I was making *The Big Bend*, for example, I wanted to darken some of the blue water areas and easily created blended colors with my colored pencils. When I put the reflected trees in the water, I colored them with a hint of blue. Remember to always test your colored pencils and blending techniques on scrap fabric pieces before adding any color directly to your art quilts.

I added a few more knots and details to these birch fabric pieces with a permanent black marker. A few black spots are sometimes all that's needed to help a white birch tree stand out.

I used blue and green colored pencils to add more realistic detail and depth to *The Big Bend*.

Stems on flowers and leaves can be very fragile. I've found if I do not cut all the bordering fabric from around a stem and leave the fabric stem a little wider, I can use a marker to color in the rest of the stem.

Light-colored flowers and fabrics have been known to dramatically change color in some of my art quilts. The orange flowers in the photo on the right below started out as pink.

You probably can't tell by looking at this photo, but my blue markers were lifesavers in fixing small gaps between some of the wave strips in this beach scene.

The stems on these plants were too thin, so I left some of the white and blue background fabric around the edges and used a green marker to fill in the extra space.

I used colored pencils and fabric markers to transform pink fabric into these lovely orange tiger lilies.

You can drastically change the colors of your fabrics using colored pencils. I liked this leaf pattern, but needed green foliage for my art quilt. Colored pencils did the trick.

Some fabrics only require minor color changes to add variety and depth to your art quilt. I used a fuchsia colored pencil to create new red tones for creating unique hummingbirds.

Fixing Pressing Errors and Splicing

There are times you may make an error in positioning when pressing a fabric piece onto the scene of the art quilt, a piece of fabric may be too small for a space, or a plant or tree might need an extra leaf or branch. Not to worry—there are some easy fixes for all these problems.

If you press a piece of fabric that is backed with fusible web to the surface of another piece of fabric, most of the time you can pick at the edges with something sharp (for example, the point of a seam ripper) and lift and move the fabric you want to reposition. Problem solved.

There are times I've collaged several pieces of fabric onto a scene, and when I go to iron them down, I realize one of the pieces is adhesive side up. This usually happens when the front and back of the fabric are almost identical. If you accidentally place a fabric piece with the adhesive side up, there's no need to rip the whole area apart and start over. Insert glue onto the back side of the backwards piece and continue working on the quilt like nothing happened. Using a glue product with a thin metal application tube (such as Roxanne Glue-Baste-It) will allow you to insert glue in very small amounts to the targeted area. After the piece is glued, use a piece of parchment paper to cover the scene before you do any additional ironing.

When a piece of fabric is too small, you might be able to splice in a matching piece to extend the size. A viewer's eye will be drawn to a straight line, so don't try to splice pieces with straight edges. To achieve the best appearance, always fussy cut the edge in an uneven manner. A viewer won't easily spot a jagged join.

Sometimes the edges of an element might be cut off at the edge of a pattern. For example, the edge of a plant might be missing. I can cut out several of these plants and collage various leaves together on parchment paper to fill in any missing parts. The same goes for trees that might need more branches—you can always splice in another branch.

Almost every time I teach a Winter Morning art quilt class, at least one person irons the pastel sky strips wrong side up. A bit of glue easily fixes the problem!

The top strip of sky was joined with a straight edge and the middle strip of sky was joined with a fussy-cut edge. You can see how the uneven edge is less noticeable.

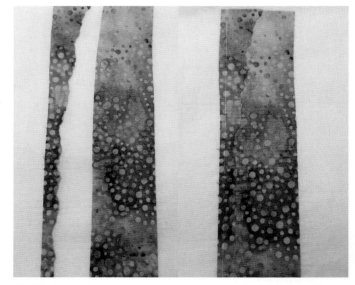

If a fabric strip is too narrow, you can widen the fabric by splicing on another piece of the same or a similar fabric. After the two pieces are pressed together, the mottled pattern dyed onto the fabric flows together.

Parchment Paper Collaging

Parchment paper is designed to be nonstick and heat resistant, which makes it perfect to use for parchment paper collaging. Because a collaged design will not permanently adhere to parchment paper, you can create design units on top of parchment paper before adhering them permanently to the background as a group. Collaged units can be peeled off the parchment paper in one complete piece. You will still back your fabric with adhesive and cut out the desired shapes, but instead of collaging them directly onto the background of your art quilt, you collage them together on the parchment paper and press them together into a unit first. Then you peel the whole piece off the parchment and add it to the background.

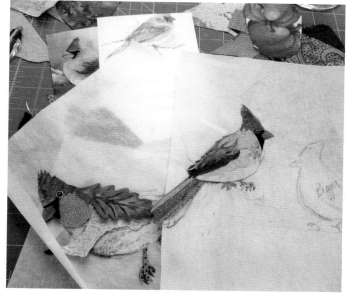

I use the parchment paper collaging technique to create cardinals and other elements that are made up of smaller fabric pieces. I sketch my design on the parchment paper, combine the pieces on top, and then press them all together.

I fussy cut these individual plant parts from some scraps of floral fabric. Once they were collaged and pressed together on parchment paper, they created a complete plant that's almost seamless.

After these pieces are pressed together on the parchment paper, they can be peeled off as whole units and added to the art quilt background.

Parchment paper collaging allows you more flexibility to create detailed items separately, then easily add them as complete units to the art quilt background.

CREATING A FLANNEL BOARD FOR PARCHMENT PAPER COLLAGING

If you plan to continue art quilting and want to incorporate parchment paper collaging, construct a simple design board you can use as both a pinning and pressing surface. You can make a sketch of the element you're working on directly onto parchment paper, pin it to the flannel board, and press the strips directly on top of the parchment paper sketch.

MATERIALS NEEDED:
- Foam poster board approximately 20" x 20" (50.8 x 50.8cm)
- Flannel that is approximately 4" (10.2cm) larger all around than the board measurements
- Cotton batting, double the size of the board for double thickness
- Large glue stick

I can sketch my design on parchment paper, then pin that paper directly to my portable flannel board to use as a workspace for building elements and pressing them together.

1. Fold the piece of batting in half.

2. Apply a few swipes of the glue stick to the front of the foam poster board and lay the folded batting on top.

3. Place the flannel face down on your work surface and apply a liberal amount of glue around the outside 2" (5.1cm) edge of the back of the flannel.

4. Place the board, batting side down, onto the center of the flannel and fold the glue-coated flannel edges around to the back of the board.

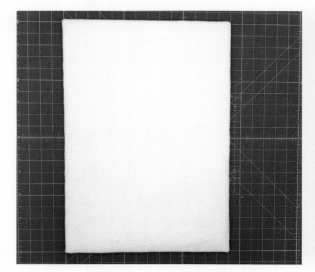

The front of my finished flannel board. Mine actually measures 14" x 20" (35.6 x 50.8cm), but I recommend making a larger one.

The back of my finished flannel board. You can see how the edges of the flannel are pulled around the edges of the foam poster board and glued down to the back.

Using Freezer Paper Templates

The first time I used a template for an element in an art quilt, I made a cardboard template and traced around it onto the fabric. This required five steps: (1) finding a reference picture or making a sketch, (2) tracing a cardboard template, (3) cutting out the cardboard template, (4) holding the template steady to keep it from shifting while I traced around it, and (5) cutting out the final fabric shape.

I soon learned that freezer paper templates are easier to use, can save a lot of time, and are more accurate. Making a freezer paper template requires fewer steps. The paper side of freezer paper is easy to draw on and because the waxy side will temporarily adhere to the fabric when pressed, you don't have to worry about holding the template in place while tracing or cutting out the fabric piece. The freezer paper template will peel off when you are finished cutting.

Creating and using cardboard templates like these seems simple enough but requires more work than using freezer paper templates.

1. Sketch the shape you want to create onto parchment paper.

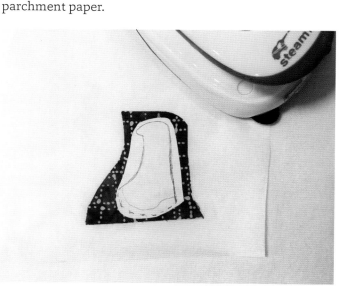

2. Pin freezer paper on top of the parchment paper sketch, paper side up, and trace the individual parts of the picture onto the freezer paper to make templates that can be cut apart. In this case, I'm creating the template for the pumpkin's stem. Roughly cut around the template, leaving some extra freezer paper around the outside edge.

3. Place a second piece of parchment paper on your ironing board to protect the ironing surface. Place the adhesive-backed fabric on this parchment paper, adhesive side down. Then place the freezer paper template in the middle of the fabric, wax side down. Then press.

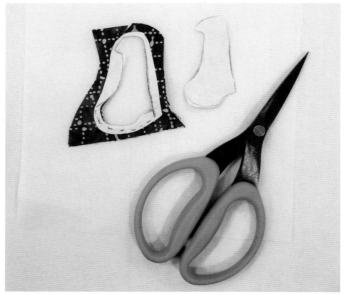

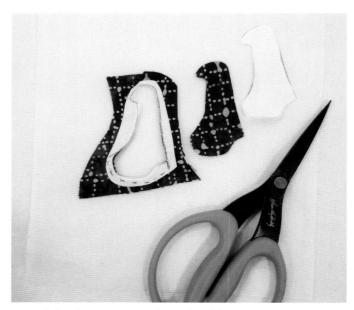

4. Allow the pressed-together fabric and freezer paper set to cool for at least 30 seconds, then peel them off the parchment paper base. Fussy cut around the template, following the lines you drew.

5. Peel the freezer paper from the fabric piece.

6. Place your original parchment paper sketch on top of the ironing board, and collage each cut out fabric piece on top, placing them where they go within the sketch. Press the whole unit together.

7. Allow the finished, pressed piece to cool and peel it off the parchment. The parchment paper collaged unit (complete with a stem made using a freezer paper template) is now ready to be added to the art quilt.

Using Printable Photo Fabric

You can include photo fabric pictures in your art quilt designs. Printing photos on printable photo fabric is like printing photos on paper. Most printable fabric sheets, such as June Tailor Sew-In Colorfast Fabric Sheets for Ink Jet Printers, will be available in US standard letter size: 8½" x 11" (21.6 x 27.9cm). You can resize and arrange saved images in programs like Microsoft Word or Photoshop, and many computer photo-viewing programs automatically allow you to adjust the printing size and number of photos per sheet directly in the printer settings. The fabric sheets feed into your printer exactly like a regular piece of paper would and you can print in color or grayscale, based on the style of your art quilt.

Printable fabric can be used to create one large image (filling the whole sheet of fabric with the image) or multiple smaller images (this could be the same image repeated if you need many small birds or leaves, for example, or it could be different images to use for several different art quilts).

Once your sheet is printed, just remove the stiffening paper from the back of the photo fabric and prepare it the same way you would prepare any other fabric for art quilting (back the whole piece with adhesive and fussy cut the individual pictures and pieces as needed).

I printed quite a few of these small cardinals on one piece of printable fabric, backed them all at the same time, and then fussy cut them all out to use for creating the *Winter Morning* scenes in these art quilts, bookmarks, and blank note cards.

This piece, *Grand Haven Pier*, 10" x 10" (25.4 x 25.4cm), includes elements that were printed in grayscale on photo fabric, including the lighthouse and the sea gulls.

The vases in these two floral arrangement pieces appear to have the reflection and texture of glass because they are images printed on photo fabric.

Projects

FLORAL FIBER ART CARDS

Once you try making one of these cards you may not be able to stop making them. They really are quite easy and so much fun to create—no sewing necessary. I'm often inspired by lovely flowers whether in real life or in paintings, photographs, or botanical sketches. After making many floral art quilts, I got the idea of pressing fabric leaves and flowers onto the front of blank cards. You'll find a lot of inspiration here for floral art cards, but once you've mastered the technique, the sky's the limit. **Note:** If you'd like to include a small vase in your arrangement, see the template on page 138.

BASIC SUPPLIES
- NO sewing machine needed
- A2 Cards—4¼" x 5½" (10.8 x 14cm) cardstock with envelopes
- Small, sharp scissors
- Tweezers
- Rotary cutter, ruler, and mat
- Iron and board
- Parchment paper or Teflon ironing sheet
- Small iron and ironing board
- Fabrics of your choice
- Printable fabric sheets for inkjet printers, such as June Tailor Sew-In Colorfast Fabric Sheets for Ink Jet Printers (optional)
- Fusible web such as Pellon 805 Wonder-Under: amount will vary
- Freezer paper: 1" x 1" (2.5 x 2.5cm) square
- Spray sizing (optional)

1. Gather together small pieces of fabrics that feature leaf or floral patterns. Also choose fabrics for any additional elements, like stems and vases. You can use designs printed on printable fabric sheets, as well. Choose your background fabrics, if desired. Stiffen all fabrics with spray sizing and back them with fusible web.

2. Fussy cut the desired elements from the fabrics, including flowers, greenery, leaves, and vases.

3. Choose one of the following three background options:

Background Option #1—a plain card; no background piece behind fussy-cut pieces/elements

Background Option #2—with fabric rectangle background behind fussy-cut pieces/elements

Background Option #3—with a multi-strip background behind fussy-cut pieces/elements

BACKGROUND OPTION #1—PLAIN CARD WITH NO BACKGROUND PIECE

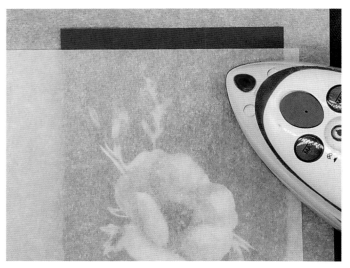

1. Place the cardstock right side up on a piece of parchment paper. Arrange the fussy-cut elements on top as desired with the adhesive side down. Gently cover with a piece of parchment paper and press.

OPTION #2—FABRIC RECTANGLE BACKGROUND

1. Cut the background fabric into a 3¼" x 4½" (8.3 x 11.4cm) rectangle. Place the cardstock right side up on a piece of parchment paper, center the fabric rectangle atop the cardstock, gently cover with a piece of parchment paper, and press.

You can make multi-strip backgrounds with more than two strips of fabric. Just make sure to square up the finished background fabric set to approximately 3¼" x 4½" (8.3 x 11.4cm). This fiber art card was based on the Tiny Tulips project on page 68.

2. Arrange the fussy-cut elements on top of the background rectangle and cardstock as desired with the adhesive side down. Gently cover with a piece of parchment paper and press.

OPTION #3—MULTI-STRIP BACKGROUND CARD

1. Cut the background fabric pieces to the desired sizes. The gray fabric in this example card was cut to 3¼" x 3½" (8.3 x 8.9cm) and the black fabric was cut to 3¼" x 1¼" (8.3 x 3.2cm).

2. Place the gray background fabric on top of a piece of parchment paper, then overlap it ¼" (6mm) with the black background fabric. Cover both with parchment paper and press. Once the set is cool, peel it from the parchment paper.

3. Use a rotary cutter and ruler to square the background fabric set to 3¼" x 4½" (8.3 x 11.4cm).

4. Place the cardstock right side up on a piece of parchment paper, center the background fabric set atop the cardstock, gently cover with a piece of parchment paper, and press.

5. Arrange the fussy-cut elements on top of the background fabric set and cardstock as desired with the adhesive side down. Gently cover with a piece of parchment paper and press.

OCEAN BOOKMARK

Outside measurement: 2¼" x 7½" (5.7 x 19.1cm)

Art quilt bookmarks are where the love of art quilting and the passion for reading converge! This project perfectly blends my first career as a teacher and literacy specialist with my second career as an art quilter. Small projects like bookmarks are great for teaching children or beginners about art quilting, and they work well to use up fabric scraps from other projects. I make a lot of bookmarks with different designs to sell at galleries and shows, to give as gifts, and to carry in my purse as tools to explain art quilting to the curious. When I found a long narrow strip of bright blue fabric, I knew it would be perfect for a bookmark showing the world of the coral reef.

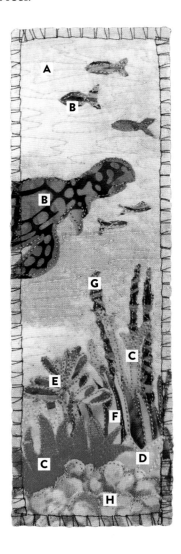

BASIC SUPPLIES

- Sewing machine (open-toe foot recommended)
- Small, sharp scissors
- Tweezers
- Rotary cutter, ruler, and mat
- Iron and board
- Teflon sheet/parchment paper
- Iron-away/erasable marking pen
- Fabrics and thread of your choice (see Fabric and Thread, below)
- Gray or medium tan bobbin thread
- Cotton backing: 2½" x 8" (6.4 x 20.3cm)
- Batting: 2½" x 8" (6.4 x 20.3cm)
  - Option 1—Fusible fleece such as Pellon TP971F Fusible Thermolam Plus or 987F Fusible Fleece
  - Option 2—Thin cotton batting
- Quilt basting spray if using thin quilt batting rather than fusible fleece
- Fusible web such as Pellon 805 Wonder-Under: approx. 5" x 10" (12.7 x 25.4cm)
- Freezer paper: approx. 2" x 5" (5.1 x 12.7cm) rectangle
- Spray sizing (optional)
- Sewing gloves (optional)

FABRIC AND THREAD

ART QUILT ELEMENT	FABRIC COLOR	MEASUREMENT	THREAD COLOR
A. Ocean background	Blue water pattern	2¼" x 7½" (5.7 x 19.1cm)	Ocean blue
B. Ocean wildlife	Printed turtle or fish patterns	2¼" x 2¼" (5.7 x 5.7cm)	Matching color
C. Plants	Red or pink	1" x 3" (2.5 x 7.6cm)	Red or pink
D. Plants	Orange or yellow	1" x 3" (2.5 x 7.6cm)	Orange or yellow
E. Plants	Bright green	1" x 3" (2.5 x 7.6cm)	Bright green
F. Plants	Medium green	1" x 3" (2.5 x 7.6cm)	Medium green
G. Plants	Dark green	1" x 3" (2.5 x 7.6cm)	Dark green
H. Ocean Floor	Tan or gray sand or rock pattern	2¼" x 1" (5.7 x 2.5cm)	Tan

1. Start making your quilt sandwich. Iron or spray together the backing and batting; either by ironing together if using fusible fleece or using quilt basting spray if using a thin cotton batting. (See Start Making the Quilt Sandwich on page 34 for additional tips.) With rotary cutter and ruler, trim the quilt sandwich to 2¼" x 7½" (5.7 x 19.1cm).

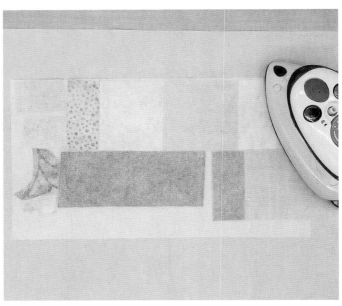

2. Choose your fabrics, press them with spray sizing (optional), and back them with iron-on adhesive.

3. Press the ocean background fabric (A) onto the fuzzy batting layer of the batting and backing set.

4. Use the matching blue thread to topstitch back and forth across the ocean background. Sew about ten wave-like lines of stitching, one every 1½" (3.8cm).

5. Fussy cut the animal and plant elements and the ocean floor (fabric pieces B–H). You can cut these freehand or use the freezer paper template technique to create templates for these pieces. See the template on page 138 and Using Freezer Paper Templates on page 55.

6. Arrange the fussy-cut animal, plant, and ocean floor pieces on top of the ocean background. Once you like the arrangement, press this layer down.

7. Topstitch just inside the outline edge of each of these fussy-cut pieces using the matching thread colors. You can work from top to bottom, or you can stitch down the most delicate elements first.

8. Press the entire bookmark with moisture, then square up the sides of the piece with a ruler and rotary cutter. Bind the edges with black thread using the blanket stitch setting on your sewing machine. This photo shows a squared-up unfinished ocean bookmark on the left and a finished one on the right .

GENERIC BOOKMARK DIRECTIONS

1. Adhere 2½" x 8" (6.4 x 20.3cm) cotton backing and batting pieces together to start the quilt sandwich. Trim to 2¼" x 7½" (5.7 x 19.1cm).

2. Back fabrics with adhesive.

3. Cut the background strips 2¼" (5.7cm) wide.

4. Press top/sky piece along the top edge of the fuzzy batting side of the quilt sandwich.

5. Fussy cut the top edges of the additional background strips.

6. Collage and arrange the rest of the background strips, starting at the top by overlapping the bottom of the top/sky piece, and layering each additional piece on top of the one before to fill space to the bottom of the batting. Press.

7. Stitch down these background strips with matching thread colors.

8. Fussy cut and add extra elements like plants, animals, or other details. Press in place.

9. Stitch down these extra elements.

10. Press with moisture.

11. Square with a rotary cutter and ruler.

12. Bind the edge with black thread using a blanket stitch setting on your sewing machine.

My *Four Seasons* designs work well mounted together as a wall hanging or as smaller bookmarks. These four examples were left with unfinished edges for mounting, but add a blanket stitch around the edges and they'd be perfect bookmarks.

Birch trees are some of my favorite art quilt subjects, and they make striking backgrounds for the small bookmark format.

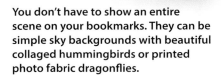

You can make bookmarks using printed photo fabric, as well. I printed the same lighthouse in color and grayscale to create two very different styles.

You don't have to show an entire scene on your bookmarks. They can be simple sky backgrounds with beautiful collaged hummingbirds or printed photo fabric dragonflies.

I made a smaller version of my standard pumpkin design and added some vines to create this whimsical bookmark.

TINY TULIPS

Outside measurement:
3" x 5" (7.6 x 12.7cm)
Inside measurement:
2¾" x 4½" (7 x 11.4cm)

I love miniatures, and I love sets of things! Art quilts capturing the different seasons are constantly on my design table. I've translated many of my seasonal art quilt designs into miniature sizes. You could always hang these like a larger art quilt or display them on small easels, but you can also attach magnets to the back and display them on the refrigerator or at work!

BASIC SUPPLIES

- Sewing machine (open-toe foot recommended)
- Small, sharp scissors
- Tweezers
- Rotary cutter, ruler, and mat
- Iron and board
- Teflon sheet/parchment paper
- Iron-away marking pen
- Large glue stick and craft/fabric glue
- Fabrics and thread of your choice (see Fabric and Thread, below)
- Printable fabric sheets for inkjet printers, such as June Tailor Sew-In Colorfast Fabric Sheets for Ink Jet Printers (optional)
- Neutral bobbin thread
- Cotton backing: 3" x 4¾" (7.6 x 12.1cm)
- Batting: 3" x 4¾" (7.6 x 12.1cm)
  - Option 1—Fusible fleece such as Pellon TP971F Fusible Thermolam Plus or 987F Fusible Fleece
  - Option 2—Thin cotton batting
- Quilt basting spray if using thin quilt batting rather than fusible fleece
- Fusible web such as Pellon 805 Wonder-Under: 3" x 14" (7.6 x 35.6cm)
- Spray sizing (optional)
- Sewing gloves (optional)
- Stretched art canvas: 3" x 5" (7.6 x 12.7cm)

FABRIC AND THREAD

ART QUILT ELEMENT	FABRIC COLOR	MEASUREMENT	THREAD COLOR
A. Sky	Light blue	2¾" x 1⅜" (7 x 3.5cm)	Light blue
B. Grass strip	Mint green	2¾" x 2½" (7 x 6.4cm)	Mint green
C. Dirt strip	Medium tan	2¾" x 1¼" (7 x 3.2cm)	Medium tan
D. Clouds	White	1" x 1" (2.5 x 2.5cm)	White
E. Tulip blooms (cut 2 or more)	Bright colors	1" x 1" (2.5 x 2.5cm) each	Matching colors
F. Tulip leaves and stems (cut 2 or more)	Medium green	2" x 2" (5.1 x 5.1cm) each	Medium green
G. Brown plant	Medium brown	1½" x 2" (3.8 x 5.1cm)	Medium brown
H. Birch trees	Birch pattern	½" x 4½" (1.3 x 11.4cm)	Gray
I. Fabric to cover stretched canvas	Kelly green	4" x 6" (10.2 x 15.2cm)	None

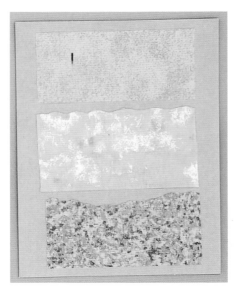

1. Start making your quilt sandwich. Iron or spray together the backing and batting; either by ironing together if using fusible fleece or using quilt basting spray if using a thin cotton batting. (See Start Making the Quilt Sandwich on page 34 for additional tips.) With rotary cutter and ruler, trim the quilt sandwich to 2¾" x 4½" (7 x 11.4cm).

2. Choose your fabrics, press them with spray sizing (optional), and back them with iron-on adhesive. Do not back the fabric for covering the canvas (I). Then fussy cut rolling edges along the tops of the grass fabric piece (B) and the dirt fabric piece (C). Wrap your stretched art canvas with the chosen fabric. See Covering a Stretched Art Canvas on page 44.

3. Place the sky fabric piece (A) onto the top of the fuzzy batting layer of the batting and backing set. Then press the fussy-cut grass piece (B) onto the middle of the fuzzy batting layer, slightly overlapping the sky fabric. Finally add the fussy-cut dirt piece (C) onto the bottom of the fuzzy batting layer, slightly overlapping the grass fabric. Gently cover with a piece of parchment paper and press.

4. Fussy cut one or two puffy cloud shapes from the cloud fabric piece (D). Add them on top of the sky piece and press. Then stitch down the background pieces and the clouds using matching threads to stitch across the outside edges and adding a few wavy lines through the background strips. **Note:** I often do minimal stitching on these mini pieces.

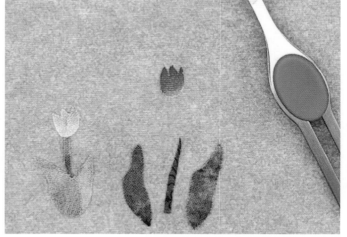

5. Fussy or rotary cut the additional elements from the other fabric pieces (E–H). You can draw these small pieces directly on the fabric with erasable pen or use freezer paper templates. Collage the tulips together on parchment paper. Place the stem and leaf pieces down first, then the tulip blooms, slightly overlapping the stem. Press together. Once they're cool, peel them from the parchment paper.

6. Arrange the trees (H), brown plant (G), and the completed tulip sets on top of the stitched-down background. Tweezers are especially helpful for arranging these miniature art quilts. Gently cover with parchment paper and press.

7. Stitch up and down the edges of the birch trees and, if you'd like, add a wavy line up the center of the trunk. For smaller projects, stitching around the outside edge of every element with matching thread is optional.

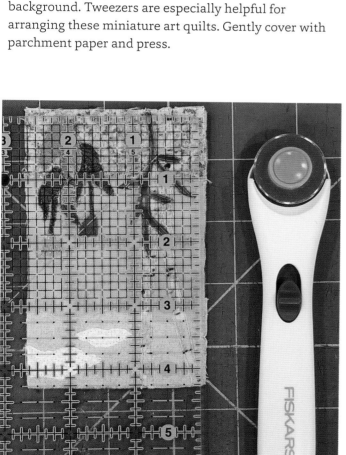

8. Press the entire scene with moisture, then square up the sides of the piece with a ruler and rotary cutter.

9. Use craft or fabric glue to mount the picture on the fabric-covered stretched art canvas.

JAKE THE DOG

Outside measurement: 12" x 9" (30.5 x 22.9cm)
Inside measurement: 10½" x 7½" (26.7 x 19.1cm)

Prepare to have fun! You will be amazed at how easy it is to incorporate a photo of your favorite pet into a simple art quilt. I've used this printable fabric to design birds and dragonflies, but I've been collecting many pictures of cute critters to experiment with in the future—racoons, skunks, rabbits, dogs, cats, and many more! This skill-building beginner project features my granddog Jake, a mix who combines popular black lab and Weimaraner traits.

I knew this photo of Jake relaxing on a beautiful day had to become an art quilt!

BASIC SUPPLIES

- Sewing machine (open-toe foot recommended)
- Small, sharp scissors
- Tweezers
- Rotary cutter, ruler, and mat
- Iron and board
- Teflon sheet/parchment paper
- Iron-away/erasable marking pen
- Large glue stick and craft/fabric glue
- Fabrics and thread of your choice (see Fabric and Thread, below)
- Printable fabric sheets for inkjet printers, such as June Tailor Sew-In Colorfast Fabric Sheets for Ink Jet Printers
- Neutral bobbin thread
- Cotton backing: 10¾" x 7¾" (27.3 x 19.7cm)
- Batting: 10¾" x 7¾" (27.3 x 19.7cm)
  - Option 1—Fusible fleece such as Pellon TP971F Fusible Thermolam Plus or 987F Fusible Fleece
  - Option 2—Thin cotton batting
- Quilt basting spray if using thin quilt batting rather than fusible fleece
- Fusible web such as Pellon 805 Wonder-Under: approx. 1 yd. (91.4cm)
- Spray sizing (optional)
- Sewing gloves (optional)
- Stretched art canvas: 12" x 9" (30.5 x 22.9cm)

Jake, like most dogs, is very photogenic. This is another photo that, thanks to printable fabric, may very well become part of a future art quilt.

TIP

Remember that the finished size of any art quilt made using photo fabric will be determined in part by the dimensions of the printable fabric sheets you use.

Jake

FABRIC AND THREAD

ART QUILT ELEMENT	FABRIC COLOR	MEASUREMENT	THREAD COLOR
A. Sky	Mottled green and teal	10½" x 5¾" (26.7 x 14.6cm)	Variegated green
B. Cement	Light tan	10½" x 6¾" (26.7 x 17.1cm)	Light tan
C. Shadow	Tan	7½" x 1½" (19.1 x 3.8cm)	Medium to light tan
D. Dog photo	Printed fabric sheet	7¾" x 6¼" (19.7 x 15.9cm)	Black, pink, and aqua
E. Flowers	Pink floral pattern	Various sizes, fussy cut	Pink
F. Stems	Medium green	2" x 5" (5.1 x 12.7cm)	Medium green
G. Green leaves	Green leaf pattern	Various sizes, fussy cut	Medium green
H. Green plant	Medium green	3" x 3" (7.6 x 7.6cm)	Medium green
I. Fabric to cover stretched canvas	Black and gray	14½" x 11½" (36.8 x 29.2cm)	None

1. Start making your quilt sandwich. Iron or spray together the backing and batting; either by ironing together if using fusible fleece or using quilt basting spray if using a thin cotton batting. (See Start Making the Quilt Sandwich on page 34 for additional tips.)
With rotary cutter and ruler, trim the quilt sandwich to 10½" x 7½" (26.7 x 19.1cm).

2. Print your photo and a name label (optional) on the printable photo fabric and remove the stiffener sheet from the back. See Using Printable Photo Fabric on page 57. Choose your other fabrics and press them with spray sizing (optional). Back all the fabrics, including the printed photo, with iron-on adhesive. Do not back the fabric for covering the canvas (I). Roughly cut the animal shape and label from the printed fabric. Wrap your stretched art canvas with the chosen fabric. See Covering a Stretched Art Canvas on page 44.

3. Fussy cut around the animal and use this piece as a guide for designing the proportions and arrangement of the background pieces. You can use erasable marker to sketch the design directly onto the quilt batting, then place the fussy-cut animal piece to one side as a reference while you work.

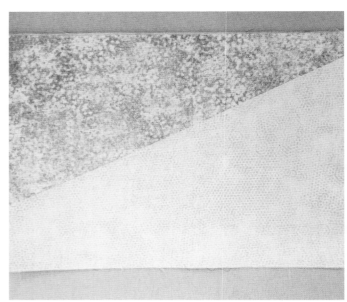

4. Use an erasable marker to mark a spot 1" (2.5cm) from the top right corner of the sky fabric piece (A) and draw a diagonal line from the bottom left corner to this spot. Mark a spot 2" (5.1cm) from the top of the cement fabric piece (B) and draw a diagonal line from the bottom left corner to this spot. Rotary cut along these lines.

5. Press the cut sky fabric piece (A) along the top edge of the fuzzy batting layer of the batting and backing set. Place the cement fabric piece (B) along the bottom edge, slightly overlapping the sky fabric piece with the cut diagonal edge of the cement fabric piece, then press.

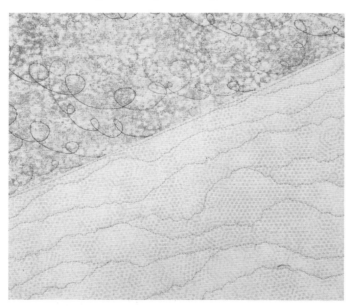

6. Using the matching thread colors, topstitch across the background pieces in patterns that match the fabric choices. In this example, I used tan thread to stitch closely across the diagonal edge of the cement, and then I stitched in a wavy pattern back and forth across the cement. For the sky, I chose variegated green thread and stitched in swirls.

7. Fussy cut the animal's shadow shape from shadow fabric piece (C). Place the cut shadow pieces down on parchment paper and align the fussy-cut fabric dog on top. Once the placement is correct, press the pieces together. After a few seconds, peel the combined dog and shadow set from the parchment paper and lightly place it on the stitched background pieces. It will still be warm and may adhere lightly to the background. (Don't press the dog down completely yet. Leaving the animal unpressed allows more flexibility when adding the floral elements.

8. Fussy cut the flower pieces (E), leaves (G), and other general plant shapes (H). Rotary cut the stem fabric piece (F) into individual stem strips approximately ¼" x 5" (6.4mm x 12.7cm).

9. If needed, use markers or colored pencils to adjust the colors of your floral fabrics to help them better match the background fabric. In this example, I changed the blue to a matching green.

10. Collage the stems, leaves, and flowers directly on top of the sky background piece. Once you are happy with the arrangement, press everything, including the dog, in place. If you are adding a name label, press it in place, as well.

11. Topstitch around the outside edges of the flowers, leaves, stems, plants, and dog using the matching thread colors. If desired, stitch around the outside of the name label, as well.

12. Press the entire scene with moisture, then square up the sides of the piece with a ruler and rotary cutter. Use craft or fabric glue to mount the picture on the fabric-covered stretched art canvas.

TIGER LILY

Outside measurement: 8" x 8" (20.3 x 20.3cm)
Inside measurement: 7" x 7" (17.8 x 17.8cm)

So many fabrics have beautiful flowers and greenery. When I was in a major floral phase with my art quilting, I searched for floral fabrics in every quilt shop I visited. Floral art quilts can develop into complex scenes or bouquets, but this project highlights the beauty of a single type of flower against a simple background.

Try creating different arrangements with your pieced-together tiger lilies. While the main project features a group of three, this piece with four has a nice balance, as well.

You can also create different lily styles by cutting lily-inspired bloom shapes from more abstract fabric pieces.

BASIC SUPPLIES

- Sewing machine (open-toe foot recommended)
- Small, sharp scissors
- Tweezers
- Rotary cutter, ruler, and mat
- Iron and board
- Teflon sheet/parchment paper
- Iron-away marking pen
- Large glue stick and craft/fabric glue
- Fabrics and thread of your choice (see Fabric and Thread, page 80)
- Neutral bobbin thread
- Cotton backing: 7¼" x 7¼" (18.4 x 18.4cm)

- Batting: 7¼" x 7¼" (18.4 x 18.4cm)
  - Option 1—Fusible fleece such as Pellon TP971F Fusible Thermolam Plus or 987F Fusible Fleece
  - Option 2—Thin cotton batting
- Quilt basting spray if using thin quilt batting rather than fusible fleece
- Fusible web such as Pellon 805 Wonder-Under: 8" x 30" (20.3 x 76.2cm)
- Spray sizing (optional)
- Sewing gloves (optional)
- Stretched art canvas: 8" x 8" (20.3 x 20.3cm)

FABRIC AND THREAD

ART QUILT ELEMENT	FABRIC COLOR	MEASUREMENT	THREAD COLOR
A. Background	Green with pattern	7" x 7" (17.8 x 17.8cm)	Light olive green
B. Leaves and stems	Light olive green	2½" x 7" (6.4 x 17.8cm)	Medium olive green
C. Leaves	Dark olive green	2½" x 7" (6.4 x 17.8cm)	Medium olive green
D. Lily blooms (cut 2 or more)	Orange lily bloom pattern	Several complete blooms	Orange and black
E. Binding	Medium green	30" x ⅞" (76.2 x 2.2cm)	Medium green
F. Fabric to cover stretched canvas	Navy	10½" x 10½" (26.7 x 26.7cm)	None

I couldn't find fabric with tiger lilies on it. Rather than using plain orange fabric, I decided to repurpose a pink floral fabric. I tested adding an orange tint using my colored pencils. Once I knew I could make it work, I backed the pink fabric with adhesive, then continued coloring before fussy cutting the flowers from the fabric.

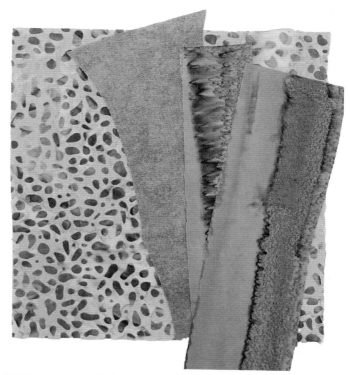

1. Start making your quilt sandwich. Iron or spray together the backing and batting; either by ironing together if using fusible fleece or using quilt basting spray if using a thin cotton batting. (See Start Making the Quilt Sandwich on page 34 for additional tips.) With rotary cutter and ruler, trim the quilt sandwich to 7" x 7" (17.8 x 17.8cm).

2. Choose your fabrics, press them with spray sizing (optional), and back them with iron-on adhesive. Do not back the fabric for covering the canvas (F). Wrap your stretched art canvas with the chosen fabric. See Covering a Stretched Art Canvas on page 44.

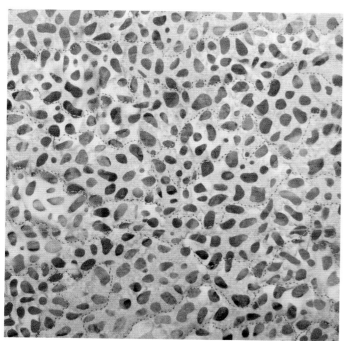

3. Place the background fabric piece (A) directly onto the fuzzy batting layer of the batting and backing set. Press, then topstitch across the background in wavy, meandering lines.

4. Rotary cut the stems and leaves from the two green fabric pieces (B and C).

5. Fussy cut the flowers from the floral fabric piece (D). You may have to adjust the shapes of the flowers to make them look more natural and realistic in your art quilt. For example, my floral fabric had rounded flower petals, so I cut pointed tips to better represent a tiger lily.

6. Collage the stems, blades, and flowers on top of the background. Carefully press the blades and stems first, lifting the edges of the lilies as you go. Only press the centers of the lilies so that stitching the leaves and stems will be easier.

7. Use a ruler and rotary cutter to trim any excess stem and leaf fabric along the bottom edge.

8. Stitch around the outlines of the leaves and stems with medium olive-green thread. Then press the entire scene, including the flower petals. Stitch the edges of the flowers with orange thread.

9. Use orange and black thread to thread paint stamens in the center of the flower.

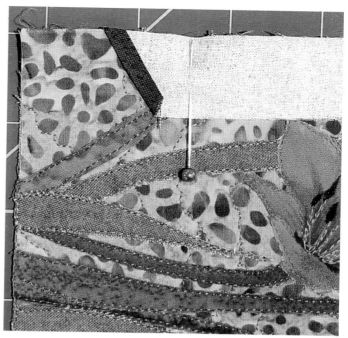

10. Press the entire scene with moisture, then square up the sides of picture with a ruler and rotary cutter. Begin stitching on the binding in the bottom left corner of the art quilt. **Note:** Cut the starting end of the strip on a diagonal and fold the edge over a scant ¼" (6.4mm). Once the binding is finished, press. For more directions, see Method Two: Adding a Binding on page 42.

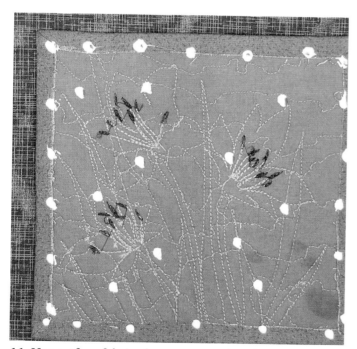

11. Use craft or fabric glue to mount the picture on the fabric-covered stretched art canvas.

Remember, once you're comfortable using the techniques, you can put your own unique spin on the designs. Create art quilts using different flower styles and in different sizes!

THE CHICKADEES

Outside measurement: 8" x 8" (20.3 x 20.3cm)
Inside measurement: 7" x 7" (17.8 x 17.8cm)

When the December snows start falling, I start designing winter birds. Cardinals are so eye-catching that they usually steal the show, but chickadees are by far the sweetest. So sweet, I couldn't include just one in this project.

Rearranging the basic pieces by removing a chickadee or swapping the pine cone to a different branch will help you make unique pieces every time.

BASIC SUPPLIES

- Sewing machine (open-toe foot recommended)
- Small, sharp scissors
- Tweezers
- Rotary cutter, ruler, and mat
- Iron and board
- Teflon sheet/parchment paper
- Iron-away marking pen
- Black permanent marker
- Silver marker or ceramic chalk pencil
- Large glue stick and craft/fabric glue
- Fabrics and thread of your choice (see Fabric and Thread, page 86)
- Neutral bobbin thread
- Cotton backing: 7¼" x 7¼" (18.4 x 18.4cm)
- Batting: 7¼" x 7¼" (18.4 x 18.4cm)
  - Option 1—Fusible fleece such as Pellon TP971F Fusible Thermolam Plus or 987F Fusible Fleece
  - Option 2—Thin cotton batting
- Quilt basting spray if using thin quilt batting rather than fusible fleece
- Fusible web such as Pellon 805 Wonder-Under: 8" x 20" (20.3 x 50.8cm)
- Freezer paper: approx. 6" x 6" (15.2 x 15.2cm) square
- Spray sizing (optional)
- Sewing gloves (optional)
- Stretched art canvas: 8" x 8" (20.3 x 20.3cm)

You can also change your pieces by adjusting your background stitching. The pieces on this page all have geometric stitching, rather than the organic stitching in the main project piece.

FABRIC AND THREAD

ART QUILT ELEMENT	FABRIC COLOR	MEASUREMENT	THREAD COLOR
A. Background	Mottled light olive green	7" x 7" (17.8 x 17.8cm)	Light olive green
B. Evergreen branches (cut 2)	Evergreen patterned fabric	3" x 1" (7.6 x 2.5cm)	Medium olive green
C. Pine cone (optional)	Pine cone patterned fabric	1" x 1" (2.5 x 2.5cm)	Medium brown or rust
D. Chickadee body bases (cut 2)	Black swirl pattern	5" x 2" (12.7 x 5.1cm)	Black
E. White collars (cut 2)	White swirl pattern	1" x ½" (2.5 x 1.3cm)	White
F. Lower Neck (cut 2)	Charcoal sparkle	1¼" x ½" (3.2 x 1.3cm)	Charcoal
G. Wings (cut 2)	Black with white pattern	1½" x ⅝" (3.8 x 1.6cm)	Black
H. Chest (cut 2)	Yellow striped	1¾" x ½" (4.4 x 1.3cm)	Light canary yellow
I. Belly (cut 2)	Pale gold or yellow	1¾" x ½" (4.4 x 1.3cm)	Light canary yellow
J. Feet (cut 2)	Charcoal batik	1" x ½" (2.5 x 1.3cm)	Charcoal (optional)
K. Tails (cut 4)	Black with white and gray stripes	2" x ¼" (5.1cm x 6.4mm)	Charcoal
L. Additional feathers (cut 4–6)	Black batik	1" x 1½" (2.5 x 3.8cm)	Black
M. Eyes	White	½" x ½" (1.3 x 1.3cm)	None
N. Fabric to cover stretched canvas	Green crosshatch	10½" x 10½" (26.7 x 26.7cm)	None

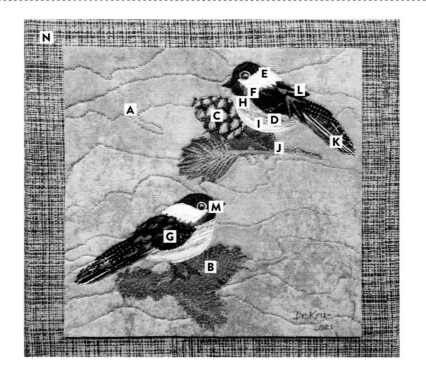

1. Start making your quilt sandwich. Iron or spray together the backing and batting; either by ironing together if using fusible fleece or using quilt basting spray if using a thin cotton batting. (See Start Making the Quilt Sandwich on page 42 for additional tips.) With rotary cutter and ruler, trim the quilt sandwich to 7" x 7" (17.8 x 17.8cm). Choose your fabrics, press them with spray sizing (optional), and back them with iron-on adhesive. Do not back the fabric for covering the canvas (N). Wrap your stretched art canvas with the chosen fabric. See Covering a Stretched Art Canvas on page 44.

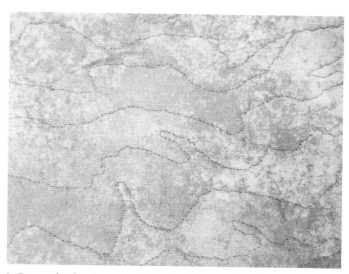

2. Press the background fabric (A) onto the fuzzy batting layer of the batting and backing set. Use the matching olive-green thread to stitch in wavy lines back and forth across the background. Set the background to the side for now.

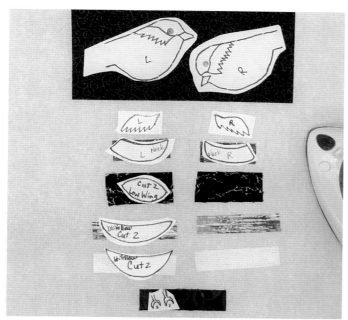

3. Trace the chickadee template pieces onto freezer paper. See templates on page 137. Use paper scissors to roughly cut out each template piece. Place a piece of parchment paper on your ironing board, then place all your fabric pieces adhesive side down on top of the parchment paper. Add the freezer paper template pieces on top of the correct fabric for each piece with the waxy side down. Press all the template pieces with the corresponding fabrics. See Using Freezer Paper Templates on page 55.

4. Fussy cut each template and fabric set, following the lines of the template. Then peel off the freezer paper templates to leave only the adhesive-backed fussy-cut fabric pieces.

5. Press the chickadee body pieces (D) onto a piece of parchment paper. Add the lower neck pieces (F), then the white collar pieces (E). Press these pieces together. See Parchment Paper Collaging on page 53 for more details.

6. Press the belly pieces (I) onto the bottom of each body piece. Then press the chest pieces (H) above and overlapping the belly pieces.

7. Press the wing pieces (G) on top of the chickadees, overlapping the lower neck and chest pieces. Set these combined chickadees aside for now.

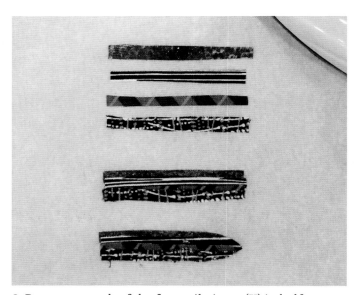

8. Rotary cut each of the four tail pieces (K) in half lengthwise. Then collage them together on top of parchment paper and press them. The strips should overlap one another. Trim one end of each tail set to a gentle point. The photo shows four separate cut strips as an example at the top, an ironed-together tail set in the middle, and an ironed-together tail set with a cut pointed end on the bottom.

9. Fussy cut four to six additional feather detail pieces (L).

10. Assemble the chickadee body sets with the tail sets and the additional fussy-cut feather pieces and press them together.

11. Use tweezers to gently lift the bottom edges of the bellies to tuck the feet in place and press.

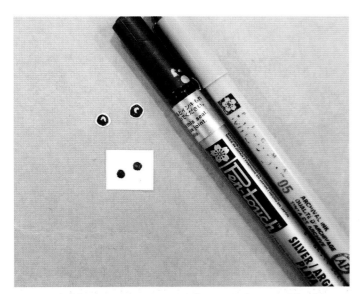

12. Use a black permanent marker to color two black dots on the small piece of white eye fabric (M), then use a silver marker or ceramic chalk pencil to draw a small, inverted *U* shape in the center of each black dot. Fussy cut around each black circle, leaving a narrow strip of white around each to create eyes.

13. Press the eyes onto the heads, slightly overlapping the white collar piece. Once the completed collaged birds are cool, carefully peel them from the parchment. (You can also add the eyes by pressing them onto the chickadees after they've been stitched down, if you prefer.)

14. Fussy cut the pine branch pieces (B) and the pine cone piece (C). (The pine cone is optional.)

15. Temporarily assemble the stitched background piece with the pine branch pieces, the pine cone piece, and the chickadees to check for correct placement. Remove the chickadees and press the pine branch pieces and pine cone piece onto the background.

16. Stitch around the edges of the pine cone with medium brown or rust thread and around the pine branches with olive-green thread. Add the chickadees back on top of the branches and press them down.

17. Stitch around the chickadees, using white thread for the white collars, yellow thread for the belly and chest, and black or charcoal thread for the upper body, tail, wings, and feet. Press the eyes in place if you haven't already done so.

18. Press the entire scene with moisture, then square up the sides of the piece with a ruler and rotary cutter. Use craft or fabric glue to mount the picture on the fabric-covered stretched art canvas.

The parchment paper collaging technique allows you to create many chickadees and use them in different ways. These pieces show just a few of the different arrangements I've tried, including an adorable ornament!

HUNTER THE HEDGEHOG

Outside measurement: 10" x 8" (25.4 x 20.3cm)
Inside measurement: 8½" x 6½" (21.6 x 16.5cm)

This was my first attempt at creating a cute critter art quilt, and the popularity of hedgehogs at present meant I had many reference pictures to inspire my design. This art quilt has a slight three-dimensional effect because the hedgehog is built on separate batting and backing pieces so he pops slightly off the background! It's a bit more complicated, but with its soft, whimsical colors and sweet subject, it is well worth the time and effort.

The hedgehog is made using parchment paper collage techniques and is then added to his own piece of batting and backing. Play around with a traditional art quilt arrangement by leaving out this extra batting and backing step.

This close-up photo really illustrates how stitching can be used not only to combine the fabrics, but also to add elements like the textured centers of the flowers.

BASIC SUPPLIES

- Sewing machine (open-toe foot recommended)
- Small, sharp scissors
- Tweezers
- Rotary cutter, ruler, and mat
- Iron and board
- Teflon sheet/parchment paper
- Iron-away marking pen
- Black permanent marker
- Silver marker or ceramic chalk pencil
- Large glue stick and craft/fabric glue
- Fabrics and thread of your choice (see Fabric and Thread, page 94)
- Neutral bobbin thread
- Cotton backing, two pieces: 8¾" x 6¾" (22.2 x 17.1cm) and 5¼" x 4¼" (13.3 x 10.8cm)

- Batting, two pieces: 8¾" x 6¾" (22.2 x 17.1cm) and 5¼" x 4¼" (13.3 x 10.8cm)
  - Option 1—Fusible fleece such as Pellon TP971F Fusible Thermolam Plus or 987F Fusible Fleece
  - Option 2—Thin cotton batting
- Quilt basting spray if using thin quilt batting rather than fusible fleece
- Fusible web such as Pellon 805 Wonder-Under: 8½" x 17" (21.6 x 43.2cm)
- Freezer Paper: 6" x 6" (15.2 x 15.2cm)
- Spray sizing (optional)
- Sewing gloves (optional)
- Stretched art canvas: 8" x 10" (20.3 x 25.4cm)

FABRIC AND THREAD

ART QUILT ELEMENT	FABRIC COLOR	MEASUREMENT	THREAD COLOR
A. Sky	Light blue	8½" x 4¾" (21.6 x 12.1cm)	Light blue
B. Ground—small floral	Sage and purple	8½" x 2" (21.6 x 5.1cm)	Light sage green
C. Small ground plants	Dark sage plant pattern	4" x 2" (10.2 x 5.1cm)	Bright green
D. Ferns or dark green plants	Fern pattern	5" x 5" (12.7 x 12.7cm)	Forest green
E. Bright green plants	Bright green plant pattern	5" x 5" (12.7 x 12.7cm)	Bright green
F. Grass blades	Sage	3" x 4½" (7.6 x 11.4cm)	Light sage green
G. Tan body	Spotted tan	4" x 2" (10.2 x 5.1cm)	Medium tan
H. Dark brown spikes	Dark brown spiky pattern	4" x 3" (10.2 x 7.6cm)	Chocolate brown
I. Small flower	Floral pattern	1½" x 1½" (3.8 x 3.8cm)	Yellow
J. Novelty bee (optional)	Novelty bee pattern	tiny	None
K. Eye, nose, and mouth (optional)	Black	¾" x ¾" (1.9 x 1.9cm)	Black
L. Fabric to cover stretched canvas	Blue	12½" x 10½" (31.8 x 26.7cm)	None

1. Start making your quilt sandwiches. Iron or spray together the backing and batting sets; either by ironing together if using fusible fleece or using quilt basting spray if using a thin cotton batting. (See Start Making the Quilt Sandwich on page 34 for additional tips.) With rotary cutter and ruler, trim the quilt sandwiches to 8½" x 6½" (21.6 x 16.5cm) and 5" x 4" (12.7 x 10.2cm).

2. Choose your fabrics, press them with spray sizing (optional), and back them with iron-on adhesive. Do not back the fabric for covering the canvas (L). Wrap your stretched art canvas with the chosen fabric. See Covering a Stretched Art Canvas on page 44.

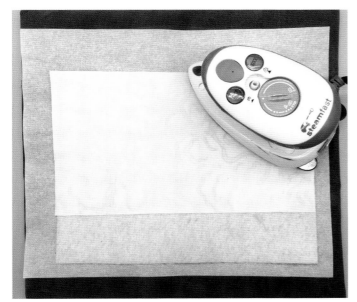

3. Press the background fabric (A) onto the top section of the fuzzy batting layer of the larger batting and backing set. Then press the background ground fabric (B) onto the bottom section of the fuzzy batting layer, slightly overlapping the sky fabric. This photo shows only the sky piece being pressed down. The ground piece will cover the batting on the bottom (see the photo in the next step).

4. Topstitch across the sky in wavy, cloud-like lines and across the ground cover in waving lines or natural lines that look like the edges of leaves or plants. **Note:** In this photo, I've already fussy cut, pressed on, and topstitched around the sage ground plant pieces (C), but it is much easier to add them later in step 13.

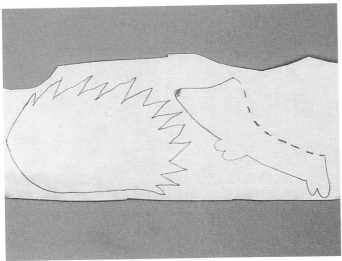

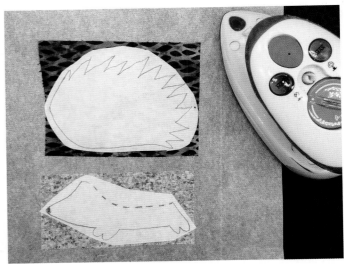

5. Trace the hedgehog template pieces onto freezer paper. See templates on page 138. The top of the lower body is a bit taller than it will appear in the finished art quilt since it will tuck under the top fur.

6. Use paper scissors to roughly cut out each template piece. Place a piece of parchment paper on your ironing board, then place your fabric pieces (G and H) adhesive-side down on top of the parchment paper. Add the freezer paper template pieces on top of the correct fabric for each piece with the waxy side down. Press all the template pieces with the corresponding fabrics. See Using Freezer Paper Templates on page 55.

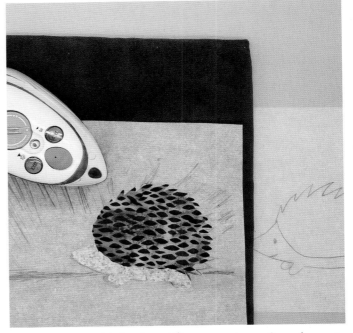

7. Fussy cut each template and fabric set, following the lines of the template. Then peel off the freezer paper template to leave only the adhesive-backed fussy-cut fabric pieces.

8. Press the tan body piece (G) onto a piece of parchment paper (notice I've sketched the basic layout of the art quilt on this piece of parchment paper). Then press the dark brown spike piece (H) on top of the body, overlapping it slightly.

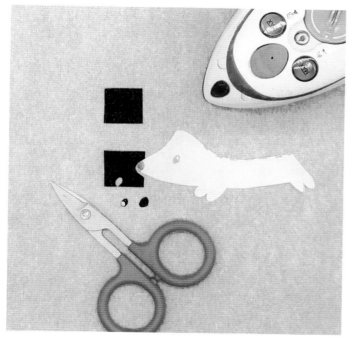

9. Fussy cut the shape of the nose and an oval for the eye from the black fabric (K). Use a black marker to add a smile and a silver marker or white ceramic chalk pencil to add a catchlight to the eye. Then press these features onto the hedgehog.

If you don't want to work with small fabric pieces to create the hedgehog's eye and nose, there are two other options. You can stitch the eye and nose using black thread, but the easiest method is to draw on these features in the same way you draw on the mouth. Use a black permanent marker to draw the nose tip and an oval for the eye, then use a silver marker or ceramic chalk pencil to add a catchlight to the eye.

10. Peel the hedgehog set off the parchment paper and press it onto the fuzzy batting layer of the smaller batting and backing set.

11. Using tan and chocolate brown threads, stitch just inside the outside edges of the hedgehog, then add spiky stitches across the dark brown fabric. This photo shows the back of the hedgehog piece to better demonstrate what these stitches look like.

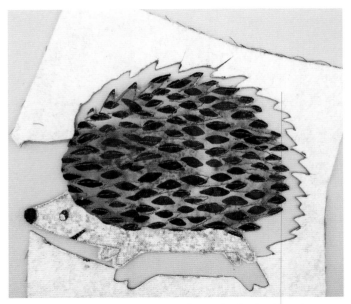

12. Cut the extra batting away from the hedgehog, just outside the stitching line. Try to bevel the cut, angling it under the hedgehog's body so no white batting is visible from the front. Set the hedgehog aside.

13. Fussy cut the plant fabric pieces (C–F), the flower piece (I), and the optional novelty bee piece (J) from the chosen fabrics. Temporarily assemble the stitched background piece with the plant pieces, the flower piece, the novelty bee piece, and the hedgehog to check for correct placement. Remove the hedgehog and press the plants onto the background.

14. Stitch around the edges of the plants and the flower centers with matching green and yellow threads. Press with moisture.

15. Add dots of craft or fabric glue on the back of the stitched hedgehog quilt sandwich, place the hedgehog where desired, then apply light pressure to glue the hedgehog to the art quilt.

16. Press the entire scene with moisture, then square up the sides of the piece with a ruler and rotary cutter. Use craft or fabric glue to mount the picture on the fabric-covered stretched art canvas.

Remember to experiment with your fabrics and shapes. These three hedgehogs all have very different personalities because of the patterned fabrics used for their spikes. I compared them all on my chosen background fabrics and ended up picking the last one to make a second hedgehog scene. The other two are ready to go for future art quilts, though!

RED POPPIES

Outside measurement:
18" x 24" (45.7 x 61cm)
Inside measurement:
16" x 22" (40.6 x 55.9cm)

Prepare to have fun again! You will amaze yourself at how easy it is to bring this vase of red poppies to life in a simple collaged art quilt. When I found this beautiful fabric poppy printed fabric, I just had to include them in an art quilt. Looking through reference images inspired me to create a still life design on a tabletop. This art quilt looks like a painting, but the fabric textures add warmth and depth.

BASIC SUPPLIES
- Basic sewing machine (open-toe foot recommended)
- Small, sharp scissors
- Tweezers
- Rotary cutter, ruler, and mat
- Iron and board
- Teflon sheet/parchment paper
- Iron-away marking pen
- Ceramic chalk pencil (optional)
- Large glue stick and craft/fabric glue
- Fabrics and thread of your choice (see Fabric and Thread, below)
- Printable fabric sheets for inkjet printers, such as June Tailor Sew-In Colorfast Fabric Sheets for Ink Jet Printers (optional)
- Neutral bobbin thread
- Cotton backing: 16¼" x 22¼" (41.3 x 56.5cm)
- Batting: 16¼" x 22¼" (41.3 x 56.5cm)
  ○ Option 1—Fusible fleece such as Pellon TP971F Fusible Thermolam Plus or 987F Fusible Fleece
  ○ Option 2—Thin cotton batting
- Quilt basting spray if using thin quilt batting rather than fusible fleece
- Fusible web such as Pellon 805 Wonder-Under: approx. 2 yd. (1.8m)
- Freezer Paper: 8" x 8" (20.3 x 20.3cm)
- Spray sizing (optional)
- Sewing gloves (optional)
- Stretched art canvas: 18" x 24" (45.7 x 61cm)

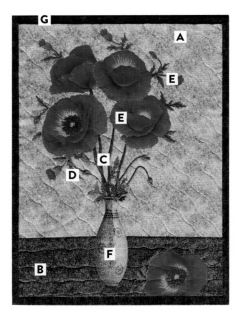

FABRIC AND THREAD

ART QUILT ELEMENT	FABRIC COLOR	MEASUREMENT	THREAD COLOR
A. Upper background	Light gray floral pattern	16" x 17" (40.6 x 43.2cm)	Light gray
B. Lower background	Black mottled or patterned	16" x 5" (40.6 x 12.7cm)	Black
C. Poppy stems	Olive green mottled	2" x 12" (5.1 x 30.5cm)	Olive green or moss
D. Poppy leaves	Serrated leaf print or olive green mottled	9" x 3½" (22.9 x 8.9cm)	Olive green or moss
E. Poppy blooms and buds (cut at least 5 large blooms and many small buds)	Floral poppy print	Various sizes	Bright red
F. Vase	Dark gray patterned or printed photo fabric image	3" x 7" (7.6 x 17.8cm)	Medium gray
G. Fabric to cover stretched canvas	Black	20½" x 26½" (52.1 x 67.3cm)	None

1. Start making your quilt sandwich. Iron or spray together the backing and batting; either by ironing together if using fusible fleece or using quilt basting spray if using a thin cotton batting. (See Start Making the Quilt Sandwich on page 34 for additional tips.) With rotary cutter and ruler, trim the quilt sandwich to 16" x 22" (40.6 x 55.9cm). Choose your fabrics, press them with spray sizing (optional), and back them with iron-on adhesive. Do not back the fabric for covering the canvas (G). Wrap your stretched art canvas with the chosen fabric. See Covering a Stretched Art Canvas on page 44. Place the upper background fabric piece (A) onto the top of the fuzzy batting layer of the batting and backing set and press. Then place the lower background fabric piece (B) onto the bottom of the fuzzy batting layer of the batting and backing set, slightly overlapping the bottom edge of the upper background fabric piece. Press.

2. Draw stitching lines to follow. On the upper background fabric piece, use an erasable pen and a ruler to mark a diagonal line from the top left corner to the bottom right corner. Continue marking diagonal lines 1" (2.5cm) apart across the entire upper background piece. It may be helpful to add freestyle wavy lines on top of these diagonal lines to follow directly when stitching but remember the sewing here doesn't have to be exact.

3. On the bottom background strip, use an erasable pen or ceramic chalk pencil and a ruler to mark three horizontal lines about 1" (2.5cm) apart. Remember that ceramic chalk will not be removed during ironing like the erasable pen will. After stitching, remove the chalk lines with water.

4. Stitch along the top edge of the lower background strip as close to the edge as you can, then stitch wavy lines along the three horizontals. On the upper background fabric, stitch wavy lines along the diagonals. Press.

TIP

Add variety to flower arrangement art quilts by using vase designs printed on printable fabric sheets. See page 57.

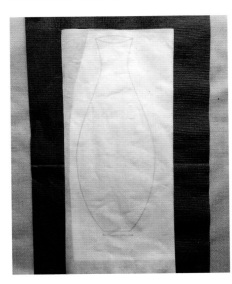

5. Trace the vase template onto freezer paper. See templates on page 138. Use paper scissors to roughly cut out the template piece. Place a piece of parchment paper on your ironing board, then place your vase fabric piece (F) adhesive side down on top of the parchment paper. Add the freezer paper template piece on top with the waxy side down and press. See Using Freezer Paper Templates on page 55.

If needed, you can create your own flower buds and blooms out of smaller parts. Collage these smaller pieces on parchment paper and press them together.

I cut these smaller parts from the same poppy print fabric. Alone they won't work within the final composition.

Collaged and pressed together, these smaller pieces become a full, lovely bloom and a decorative bud.

6. Fussy cut the leaves and poppies from the leaf and poppy fabric pieces (D and E). Rotary cut the stem fabric (C) into thin strips.

7. Arrange the vase, stems, leaves, and poppies on top of the background, making it appear as though the vase is resting on top of the "table" created by the lower background piece. Once you are happy with the arrangement, press. **Note:** It's possible to bend a straight stem by curving it as you press, working from bottom to top.

8. Stitch around the outside edges of the vase, stems, leaves, and poppies. Then fussy stitch details into the flower centers.

9. Press the entire scene with moisture, then square up the sides of the piece with a ruler and rotary cutter. Use craft or fabric glue to mount the picture on the fabric-covered stretched art canvas.

OVER THE CATTAILS

Outside measurement: 10" x 8" (25.4 x 20.3cm)
Inside measurement: 9" x 7" (22.9 x 17.8cm)

This art quilt design began when one of my good friends took a picture of a loon and asked for my advice on how to use it as a wall hanging. I enlarged the loon picture to 8" x 10" (20.3 x 25.4cm) and printed it on photo fabric, then I fussy cut and collaged pond flowers, grasses, and cattails to surround the loon. I liked the resulting arrangement of greenery so much, I asked permission from my friend to use the concepts to create my own series of cattail art quilts.

Try machine stitching cattail tips on with golden or tan thread instead of using small fabric pieces to see which style you prefer.

This close-up photo shows how important layering and variety are in this project. Mixing many different textures and shades of color will help your finished piece better mimic a natural scene.

BASIC SUPPLIES

- Sewing machine (open-toe foot recommended)
- Small, sharp scissors
- Tweezers
- Rotary cutter, ruler, and mat
- Iron and board
- Teflon sheet/parchment paper
- Iron-away marking pen
- Large glue stick and craft/fabric glue
- Fabrics and thread of your choice (see Fabric and Thread, page 106)
- Neutral bobbin thread
- Cotton backing: 9¼" x 7¼" (23.5 x 18.4cm)
- Batting: 9¼" x 7¼" (23.5 x 18.4cm)
  - Option 1—Fusible fleece such as Pellon TP971F Fusible Thermolam Plus or 987F Fusible Fleece
  - Option 2—Thin cotton batting
- Quilt basting spray if using thin quilt batting rather than fusible fleece
- Fusible web such as Pellon 805 Wonder-Under: 1 yd. (91.4cm)
- Spray sizing (optional)
- Sewing gloves (optional)
- Stretched art canvas: 8" x 10" (20.3 x 25.4cm)

FABRIC AND THREAD

ART QUILT ELEMENT	FABRIC COLOR	MEASUREMENT	THREAD COLOR
A. Sky	Light teal	9" x 4½" (22.9 x 11.4cm)	Light teal
B. Water	Medium teal	9" x 3" (22.9 x 7.6cm)	Clear iridescent
C. Dark teal waves	Dark teal	5" x ½" (12.7 x 1.3cm)	Clear iridescent
D. Moon	Pale yellow	1¼" x 1¼" (3.2 x 3.2cm)	Pale yellow
E. White clouds	White	5" x ½" (12.7 x 1.3cm)	White
F. Peach clouds	Peach	5" x ½" (12.7 x 1.3cm)	Peach
G. Brown cattails	Dark brown mottled	1½" x ¾" (3.8 x 1.9cm)	Dark brown
H. Green cattail stems	Medium olive green	2" x 5" (5.1 x 12.7cm)	Medium olive green
I. Cattail tip	Tan tweed	⅝" x ¼" (1.6cm x 6.4mm)	None
J. Green plants	Various green batik plant patterns	Various up to 3½" (8.9cm) tall	Matching greens
K. Brown plants	Various brown batik plant patterns	Various up to 2" (5.1cm) tall	Matching browns
L. Red flowers	Red with sparkles	3" x ¼" (7.6cm x 6.4mm)	None
M. Geese (optional)	Goose pattern	1" x 1" (2.5 x 2.5cm)	None
N. Fabric to cover stretched canvas	Black	12½" x 10½" (31.8 x 26.7cm)	None

1. Start making your quilt sandwich. Iron or spray together the backing and batting; either by ironing together if using fusible fleece or using quilt basting spray if using a thin cotton batting. (See Start Making the Quilt Sandwich on page 34 for additional tips.) With rotary cutter and ruler, trim the quilt sandwich to 9" x 7" (22.9 x 17.8cm).

2. Choose your fabrics, press them with spray sizing (optional), and back them with iron-on adhesive. Do not back the fabric for covering the canvas (N). Wrap your stretched art canvas with the chosen fabric. See Covering a Stretched Art Canvas on page 44.

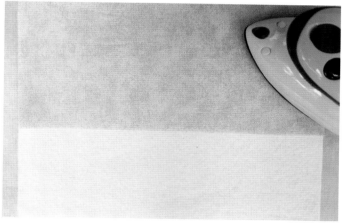

3. Place the sky fabric piece (A) onto the top of the fuzzy batting layer of the batting and backing set. Press. I topstitched the sky in the example quilt after a later step, but it would be helpful to topstitch the sky with wavy, cloud-like lines now.

4. Use a quarter as a template to trace and cut a round circle or a sliver of the round circle from the moon fabric piece (D). Add the moon on top of the sky fabric piece and press. I topstitched the moon in the example quilt after a later step, but it would be helpful to topstitch the outline of the moon now.

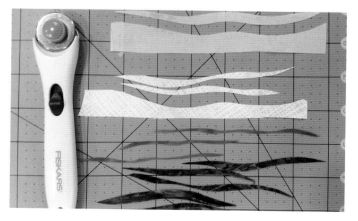

5. Rotary cut a few strips of the cloud fabric pieces (E and F). To save time later, rotary cut strips from the dark teal wave fabric piece (C). Set the dark teal waves to the side.

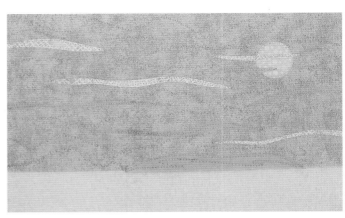

6. Arrange the white and peach clouds across the sky and moon and press.

7. In the example quilt, I stitched down the sky and moon at this point. You should already have topstitched the sky and the moon in earlier steps, but if not, stitch them now. Then stitch around the outside edges of the clouds.

8. Place the water fabric piece (B) on the bottom of the fuzzy batting layer of the batting and backing set, slightly overlapping the bottom of the sky fabric. Press. Arrange the dark teal wave pieces rotary cut earlier on top of the water and press.

9. Stitch across the water and around the outside edges of the dark teal waves using iridescent thread.

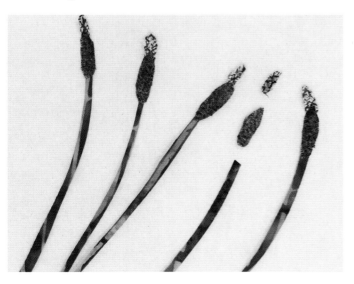

10. Fussy cut the cattail fabric pieces (G–I). Cattail shapes are easy to make. Cut three to five short, narrow strips from the brown fabric (G), then trim off each corner of the strip so that it resembles a hotdog. Rotary cut long, narrow strips of the green fabric (H) for the stems. Cut short turfs of the tan tweed fabric (I). Collage and press these three parts together atop parchment paper to construct each cattail.

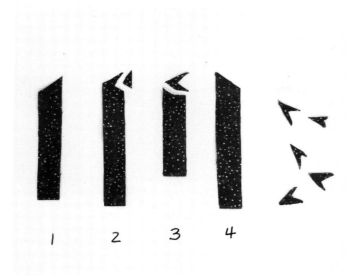

11. Fussy cut various plants from the green and brown plant-patterned batik fabric pieces (J and K). Fussy cut small red flower buds that resemble Indian Paint or Cardinal Flowers from the red fabric piece (L) as shown. These are fragile, so set them aside to add to the art quilt later.

12. Fussy cut the geese from the patterned fabric piece (M) and press them onto the art quilt.

TIP

If you don't want to work with tiny fussy-cut fabric geese, you can draw or stitch them instead. First, draw small geese onto the sky with an erasable pen, then either darken them with a permanent marker or stitch them on with black thread.

13. Arrange the fussy-cut plants across the bottom edge of the scene and press just the lower edges. Leave the top edges free to be able to easily tuck the cattails behind them. Add the cattails to the scene.

14. Trim the cattails and tuck them beneath the top edges of the plants. Press the plants and cattails.

15. Stitch down the plants and cattails with matching threads.

16. Add and press the fussy-cut red flowers onto the scene—no stitching necessary.

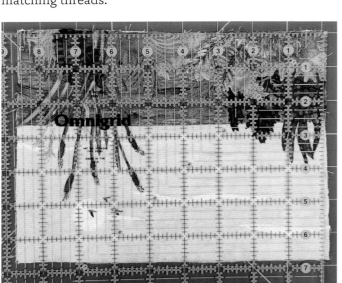

17. Press the entire scene with moisture, then square up the sides of the piece with a ruler and rotary cutter.

18. Use craft or fabric glue to mount the picture on the fabric-covered stretched art canvas.

Try other variations on the cattails theme. In this version, I left more of the water layer visible, included some smaller trees and shrubs, and worked in some more realistic geese. It still includes the natural layering of the wetlands scene, with a few unique twists.

SPRING TRILLIUM

Outside measurement: 10" x 10" (25.4 x 25.4cm)
Inside measurement: 9" x 9" (22.9 x 22.9cm)

A beautiful close-up photo of a single spring trillium bloom inspired the *Spring Trillium* design. The photo focused on the flower, leaving the background in a soft haze. To translate the mood of the picture and that hazy effect into an art quilt, I used the back sides of a few of my fabrics to create the background. Many Michiganders are lovers of our white spring trillium, and after I see them blooming in the woods each spring, a new trillium art quilt design always seems to pop up on my design table.

BASIC SUPPLIES

- Sewing machine (open-toe foot recommended)
- Small, sharp scissors
- Tweezers
- Rotary cutter, ruler, and mat
- Iron and board
- Teflon sheet/parchment paper
- Iron-away marking pen
- Large glue stick and craft/fabric glue
- Fabrics and thread of your choice (see Fabric and Thread, page 114)
- Neutral bobbin thread
- Cotton backing: 9¼" x 9¼" (23.5 x 23.5cm)
- Batting: 9¼" x 9¼" (23.5 x 23.5cm)
  - Option 1—Fusible fleece such as Pellon TP971F Fusible Thermolam Plus or 987F Fusible Fleece
  - Option 2—Thin cotton batting
- Quilt basting spray if using thin quilt batting rather than fusible fleece
- Fusible web such as Pellon 805 Wonder-Under: 1 yd. (91.4cm)
- Freezer Paper: 8" x 8" (20.3 x 20.3cm) square
- Spray sizing (optional)
- Sewing gloves (optional)
- Stretched art canvas: 10" x 10" (25.4 x 25.4cm)

The trillium design can be simplified and adapted to work on the smaller scale of bookmarks, as well. See Generic Bookmark Directions on page 66.

The fabric you choose to cover the stretched art canvas can make all the difference in the finished piece. This brighter green gives a very different energy than the mottled black used for the main project.

FABRIC AND THREAD

ART QUILT ELEMENT	FABRIC COLOR	MEASUREMENT	THREAD COLOR
A. Sky	Light blue	9" x 5" (22.9 x 12.7cm)	Light blue
B. Misty bushes	Mint green	8" x 4¾" (20.3 x 12.1cm)	Mint green
C. Low bushes	Dark olive green	9" x 1¾" (22.9 x 4.4cm)	Dark olive green
D. Groundcover	Tans	9" x 3½" (22.9 x 8.9cm)	Medium tan
E. Brown trees	Chocolate brown (back side)	3½" x 6½" (8.9 x 16.5cm)	Chocolate brown
F. Blue trees	Slate blue (back side)	3" x 5" (7.6 x 12.7cm)	Slate blue
G. Trillium leaves	Olive green	6" x 3" (15.2 x 7.6cm)	Medium olive green
H. Trillium petals	White with swirl pattern	7" x 1¾" (17.8 x 4.4cm)	White embroidery floss
I. Trillium flower center, optional	Yellow	½" x ½" (1.3 x 1.3cm)	Bright yellow
J. Small green plants (cut 10–12)	Various pale green and sage fabrics	Various 1" x 1" (2.5 x 2.5cm) and 1" x 1½" (2.5 x 3.5cm) each	Matching pale green and sage threads
K. Twigs (cut two)	Chocolate brown twig-patterned batik	1½" x 3" (3.8 x 7.6cm) each	Medium brown
L. Fabric to cover stretched canvas	Black	12½" x 12½" (31.8 x 31.8cm)	None

1. Start making your quilt sandwich. Iron or spray together the backing and batting; either by ironing together if using fusible fleece or using quilt basting spray if using a thin cotton batting. (See Start Making the Quilt Sandwich on page 34 for additional tips.) With rotary cutter and ruler, trim the quilt sandwich to 9" x 9" (22.9 x 22.9cm).

2. Choose your fabrics, press them with spray sizing (optional), and back them with iron-on adhesive. Do not back the fabric for covering the canvas (L). Wrap your stretched art canvas with the chosen fabric. See Covering a Stretched Art Canvas on page 44.

3. Place the sky fabric piece (A) onto the top of the fuzzy batting layer of the batting and backing set and press.

4. Fussy cut large background bushes from the mint fabric piece (B) and press them onto the sky.

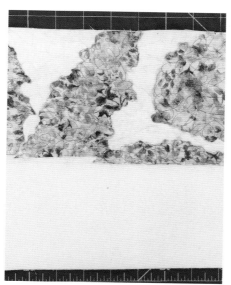

5. Use matching thread to topstitch the sky with wavy cloud-like lines and the bushes with swirling loops.

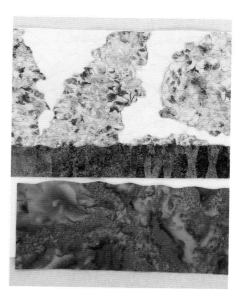

6. Cut rolling edges on top of both the dark olive fabric piece (C) and the ground cover fabric piece (D). Press the dark olive strip onto the art quilt surface, slightly overlapping the sky and bushes. Press the ground cover strip onto the bottom of the art quilt surface, slightly overlapping the dark olive strip.

7. Fussy stitch the dark olive strip across the top and in jagged spikes. Stitch the ground cover with rolling rocky lines. This photo shows the stitching from the back of the art quilt.

8. Use a rotary cutter to cut four or more tall, narrow trees from the brown tree fabric piece (E) and six or more tall, narrower trees from the blue tree fabric piece (F). Arrange these trees on top of the art quilt background, placing the blue trees so they look like they're growing out from behind the dark olive strip and extending the brown trees into the ground cover strip.

9. Stitch down the trees with matching threads by stitching around the outside edges and adding bark-like lines up the middles of the trunks. This photo shows the stitching from the back of the art quilt.

10. Trace the trillium template pieces onto freezer paper. See templates on page 139. Use paper scissors to roughly cut out each template piece. Place a piece of parchment paper on your ironing board, then place your trillium fabric pieces (G–I) adhesive side down on top of the parchment paper. Add the freezer paper template pieces on top of the correct fabric for each piece with the waxy side down. Press all the template pieces with the corresponding fabrics. Once they are cool, fussy cut each template/fabric set and remove the freezer paper. See Using Freezer Paper Templates on page 55.

11. Once all the trillium pieces are cut out, arrange them on top of a piece of parchment paper and press them together. When cool, peel the trillium unit from the parchment paper. **Note:** I did not include the optional yellow center in this example quilt.

12. Fussy cut plants and twigs from your chosen fabrics (J and K).

13. Arrange the trillium unit, the small plants, and the twigs on the art quilt background and press.

14. Use an erasable pen to draw stitching lines onto the flower petals and larger leaves. **Note:** I looked at several reference pictures from the internet to visualize the patterns on the petals and leaves.

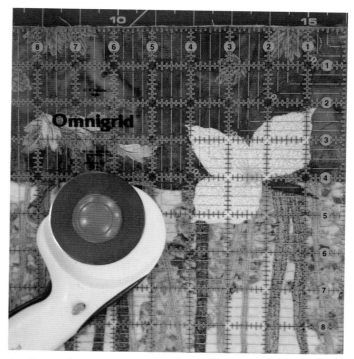

15. Stitch the outlines of the plants, twigs, and the trillium. Stitch along the erasable pen lines drawn in the previous step. Stitch the center of the flower. **Note:** In this example, I've created the center of the flower with stitching. If you use the optional yellow fabric, stitch around the outside, then add a similar asterisk shape in the middle.

16. Press the entire scene with moisture, then square up the sides of the piece with a ruler and rotary cutter. Use craft or fabric glue to mount the picture on the fabric-covered stretched art canvas.

MISS DRAGONFLY

Outside measurement: 12" x 16" (30.5 x 40.6cm)
Inside measurement: 10" x 14" (25.4 x 35.6cm)

During the winter I spend design time creating and teaching art quilting classes using winter bird designs. The programming director at my local quilt shop saw them and requested a class for a dragonfly. The timing was perfect: as the new growth and warm weather of spring came to life, so did my *Miss Dragonfly* design.

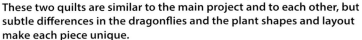

These two quilts are similar to the main project and to each other, but subtle differences in the dragonflies and the plant shapes and layout make each piece unique.

Simplify the dragonfly design and pare down the number of plants you include to create a small-scale bookmark art piece! See Generic Bookmark Directions on page 66.

BASIC SUPPLIES

- Sewing machine (open-toe foot recommended)
- Small, sharp scissors
- Tweezers
- Rotary cutter, ruler, and mat
- Iron and board
- Teflon sheet/parchment paper
- Iron-away marking pen
- Large glue stick and craft/fabric glue
- Temporary basting glue such as Roxanne Glue-Baste-It
- Fabrics and thread of your choice (see Fabric and Thread, page 120)
- Neutral bobbin thread
- Two sequins or gems for eyes

- String of pearl beads: 2" (5.1cm) long
- Cotton backing: 10¼" x 14¼" (26 x 36.2cm)
- Batting: 10¼" x 14¼" (26 x 36.2cm)
  - Option 1—Fusible fleece such as Pellon TP971F Fusible Thermolam Plus or 987F Fusible Fleece
  - Option 2—Thin cotton batting
- Quilt basting spray if using thin quilt batting rather than fusible fleece
- Fusible web such as Pellon 805 Wonder-Under: approx. 1 yd. (91.4cm)
- Freezer paper: approx. 6" x 6" (15.2 x 15.2cm) square
- Spray sizing (optional)
- Sewing gloves (optional)
- Stretched art canvas: 12" x 16" (30.5 x 40.6cm)

FABRIC AND THREAD

ART QUILT ELEMENT	FABRIC COLOR	MEASUREMENT	THREAD COLOR
A. Sky	Olive green mottled	10" x 10¼" (25.4 x 26cm)	Olive green
B. Water	Blue-purple batik	10" x 4" (25.4 x 10.2cm)	Orchid
C. Dark purple waves	Dark purple mottled	9" x 1" (22.9 x 2.5cm)	Medium purple
D. Blue-purple waves	Purple/aqua batik	9" x 1" (22.9 x 2.5cm)	Orchid
E. White or cream seeded plants	White or cream batik with seeded plants	6" x 7" (15.2 x 17.8cm)	Olive green
F. Dark green plants (cut 3)	Dark green batik with curly plants	3" x 5" (7.6 x 12.7cm)	Forest green
G. Lime green plant (cut 2)	Lime dot patterned	2" x 2" (5.1 x 5.1cm)	Lime green
H. Dark purple flowers	Dark purple mottled batik	2" x 2" (5.1 x 5.1cm)	Dark purple
I. Orchid purple flowers (cut 6)	Orchid floral batik	varies	Orchid
J. Grass blades	Dark olive stripe pattern	2½" x 11" (6.4 x 27.9cm)	Dark olive green
K. Cattail stems	Medium olive green	¾" x 9" (1.9 x 22.9cm)	Olive green
L. Bright green cattails	Bright green tone-on-tone	2" x 2⅜" (5.1 x 6cm)	Lime green
M. Gold or brown cattail tips (optional)	Gold or tan stripes	1" x ½" (2.5 x 1.3cm)	Gold metallic
N. Four-wing piece	Olive, green, orchid patterned	4¼" x 1¼" (10.8 x 3.2cm)	None
O. Upper wings	Lime green satin	4¼" x 1" (10.8 x 2.5cm)	None
P. Lower wings	Sage green satin	4¼" x 1" (10.8 x 2.5cm)	None
Q. Dark green body	Dark green batik	½" x 3¼" (1.3 x 8.3cm)	None
R. Dark purple body	Dark purple mottled batik	¼" x 2½" (6.4mm x 6.4cm)	None
S. Purple tulle wings	Dark purple tulle	2" x 2½" (5.1 x 6.4cm)	None
T. Novelty dragonflies (cut 2–3)	Purple or teal	3"–4" (7.6–10.2cm) long	None
U. Fabric to cover stretched canvas	Teal geometric	14½" x 18½" (36.8 x 47cm)	None

1. Start making your quilt sandwich. Iron or spray together the backing and batting; either by ironing together if using fusible fleece or using quilt basting spray if using a thin cotton batting. (See Start Making the Quilt Sandwich on page 34 for additional tips.) With rotary cutter and ruler, trim the quilt sandwich to 10" x 14" (25.4 x 35.6cm).

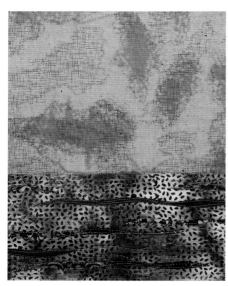

4. Topstitch across the sky in a cloud-like pattern and across the water and around the edges of the wave strips with matching thread colors. Set this stitched background to the side.

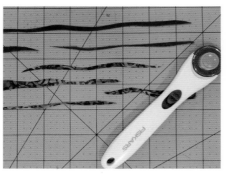

2. Choose your fabrics, press them with spray sizing (optional), and back them with iron-on adhesive. Do not back the fabric for covering the canvas (U). Wrap your stretched art canvas with the chosen fabric. See Covering a Stretched Art Canvas on page 44. Rotary cut the dark purple fabric (C) and blue-purple fabric (D) into wave-like slivers and set them aside.

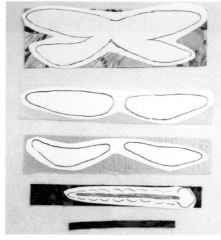

5. Trace the dragonfly template pieces onto freezer paper. See templates on page 137. Use paper scissors to roughly cut out each template piece. Place a piece of parchment paper on your ironing board, then place your fabric pieces (N–Q) adhesive side down on top of the parchment paper. Add the freezer paper template pieces on top of the correct fabric for each piece with the waxy side down. Press all the template pieces with the corresponding fabrics. See Using Freezer Paper Templates on page 55.

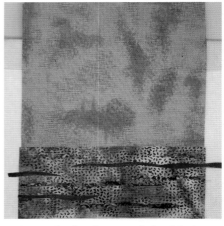

3. Press the background sky fabric (A) onto the top of the fuzzy batting layer of the batting and backing set. Then press the background water fabric (B) onto the bottom section of the fuzzy batting layer, slightly overlapping the sky fabric. Finally add the dark purple and blue-purple waves cut in step 2 on top of the water fabric (B) as desired. Press them down.

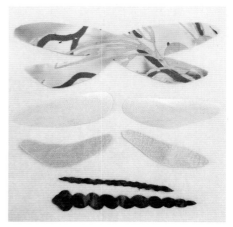

6. Fussy cut each template and fabric set, following the lines of the template. Then peel off the freezer paper template to leave only the adhesive-backed fussy-cut fabric pieces. Fussy cut small, scalloped edges around the dark purple body piece (R).

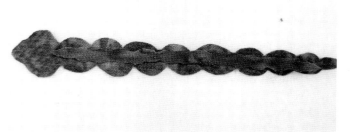

7. Press the dark green body piece (Q) onto a piece of parchment paper. Then press the dark purple body piece (R) on top of the body. Once it's cool, peel it from the parchment paper and set it aside.

8. Press only the top edge of the four-wing piece (N) onto a piece of parchment paper.

9. Slide the lower wing pieces (P) beneath the bottom edge of the four-wing set and press them down. Place the green and purple body set in the center of the wings and press down only the head.

10. Cut two corners off the purple tulle pieces (S) to create one curved edge on each. Pinch together the square end of one piece of purple tulle and slide this pinched-together end beneath the green body piece (Q) on top of the four-wing piece (N). Carefully press down the body on that side. Then repeat for the other wing.

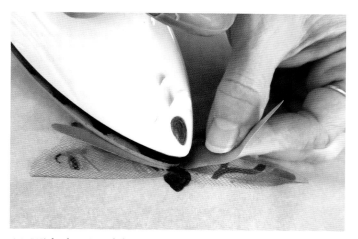

11. With the tip of the iron, press down just the inside edges of the lime green upper wing pieces (O) on top of the green and purple body set.

12. Apply two small dots of craft or fabric glue on the dragonfly's head and press one sequin on each. Apply a thin strip of craft or fabric glue along the dragonfly's back and press the pearl bead strip into the glue. Set the dragonfly aside.

13. Fussy cut the plant pieces (E–G), the flower pieces (H and I), and the novelty dragonfly pieces (T).

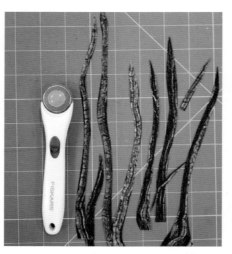

14. Rotary cut the grass pieces (J) into strips and cut pointed tips on one end.

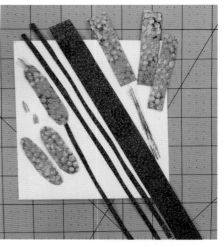

15. Rotary cut three narrow strips of the cattail stem fabric (K). Cut three strips of the bright green cattail fabric (L) and trim each corner off to create a hotdog shape. Rotary cut the cattail tip fabric (M) to create short, pointed tufts.

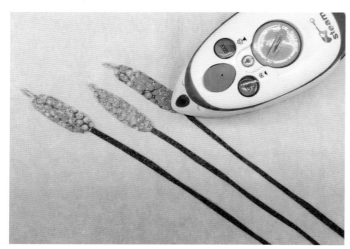

16. Press the cut stem pieces onto a piece of parchment paper. Then arrange the bright green cattails and the tan cattail tips. The bright green cattails should slightly overlap both the stems and the tips. Press everything together. Once the cattails are cool, peel them from the parchment paper.

TIP

If you'd rather not work with the small pieces of fabric needed for the cattail tips, these can be added later by machine stitching them with gold thread.

17. Begin adding the cattails and other plants to the background, layering them as desired. The lower plants should cover the bottoms of the cattail stems.

18. Topstitch the edges of the plants in matching green threads. Stitch the edges of the flowers in matching purple threads.

19. Press the entire scene with moisture, then square up the sides of the piece with a ruler and rotary cutter.

20. Before mounting the art quilt to the fabric-covered stretched art canvas, use it to determine where to press the fussy-cut fabric novelty dragonflies (T). Once you've decided on placement, set the art quilt aside and press down the novelty dragonfly pieces.

21. Use craft or fabric glue to mount the picture on the fabric-covered stretched art canvas, overlapping the novelty dragonflies.

22. Use craft or fabric glue to attach the completed dragonfly unit onto the scene.

RISE & SHINE!

Outside measurement: 16" x 20" (40.6 x 50.8cm)
Inside measurement: 11¾" x 15¾" (29.8 x 40cm)

My brother and sister-in-law invited me to visit them at their winter home on the Hawaiian island of Kauai. The first things to catch my eye were the fabulously colored roosters pecking around everywhere. Having been scattered by 1992's devastating Hurricane Iniki, they roam free-range to this day. Of all the projects in this book, Rise & Shine! earns the "most challenging" award because of its size, the number of different fabrics used, and the improvisational nature of the fussy cutting.

One thing that surprised me about my trip to Hawaiian island Kauai was the abundance of brilliantly colored roosters—they seemed to be everywhere! My photo of this fellow's regal beauty was one of many images I used to inspire a unique art quilt to remember my trip.

BASIC SUPPLIES
- Sewing machine (open-toe foot recommended)
- Small, sharp scissors
- Tweezers
- Rotary cutter, ruler, and mat
- Iron and board
- Teflon sheet/parchment paper
- Iron-away marking pen
- Silver marker or ceramic chalk pencil
- Large glue stick and craft/fabric glue
- Fabrics and thread of your choice (see Fabric and Thread, page 128)
- Neutral bobbin thread
- Cotton backing: 12¼" x 16¼" (30.5 x 40.6cm)

- Batting: 12¼" x 16¼" (30.5 x 40.6cm)
  - Option 1—Fusible fleece such as Pellon TP971F Fusible Thermolam Plus or 987F Fusible Fleece
  - Option 2—Thin cotton batting
- Quilt basting spray if using thin quilt batting rather than fusible fleece
- Fusible web such as Pellon 805 Wonder-Under: 2–3 yds. (2–3m)
- Freezer paper: approx. 8½" x 11" (21.6 x 27.9cm) rectangle
- Spray sizing (optional)
- Sewing gloves (optional)
- Stretched art canvas: 16" x 20" (40.6 x 50.8cm)

FABRIC AND THREAD

ART QUILT ELEMENT	FABRIC COLOR	MEASUREMENT	THREAD COLOR*
A. Sky	Aqua cloud pattern	12" x 10" (30.5 x 25.4cm)	Light aqua (#53)
B. Sun	Gold with gems	6" x 1½" (15.2 x 3.8cm)	Gold (#7005)
C. Small green plants (cut at least 6)	Dark green batik with plant pattern	1" x 1" (2.5 x 2.5cm)	Green (#237)
D. Flower	Floral pattern	1½" x 2" (3.8 x 5.1cm)	Pastel green (#152)
E. Peach grass	Peach and salmon batik with twig pattern	5" x 3" (12.7 x 7.6cm)	Coral (#80)
F. Sand	Tan sparkle	12" x 5" (30.5 x 12.7cm)	Light tan (#198)
G. Brown pebbles	Brown spotted batik	12" x 3½" (30.5 x 8.9cm)	Maple brown (#19)
H. Corn grass	Rust-colored spotted batik	7" x 2½" (17.8 x 6.4cm)	Light copper (#612)
I. Lime green grass	Lime green grass pattern	7" x 1¾" (17.8 x 4.4cm)	Pastel green (#152)
J. Outside eye area	Red	1" x ¾" (2.5 x 1.9cm)	Red (#367)
K. Eye pupil	Black	½" x ½" (1.3 x 1.3cm)	Black (#0)
L. Eye iris	Canary yellow	½" x ½" (1.3 x 1.3cm)	Canary yellow (#578)
M. Eye white	White	1" x ¾" (2.5 x 1.9cm)	White (#111)
N. Beak and feet	Dark yellow (saffron)	2½" x 2½" (6.4 x 6.4cm)	Dark yellow (#417)
O. Comb and wattle	Pink mottled	3" x 3" (7.6 x 7.6cm)	Red (#367)
P. Head and neck	Orange	2⅕" x 3" (6.4 x 7.6cm)	Orange (#351)
Q. Upper neck ruff	Orange floral batik	4½" x 2" (11.4 x 5.1cm)	Orange (#351)
R. Lower neck ruff	Multicolored tan and teal batik	4½" x 1" (11.4 x 2.5cm)	Medium beige (#215)
S. Chest and legs	Medium green spotted batik	5¼" x 5¼" (13.3 x 13.3cm)	Dark green (#707)
T. Upper wing	Green mottled	2" x 3" (5.1 x 7.6cm)	Green (#237)
U. Lower wing	Dark teal tone on tone	2¼" x 4" (5.7 x 10.2cm)	Stone blue (#903)
V. Top back feathers	Multicolored paint pattern	3½" x 2" (8.9 x 5.1cm)	Medium teal (#385)
W. First row tail feathers	Dark royal blue swirl	1½" x 6" (3.8 x 15.2cm)	Royal blue (#232)
X. Second row tail feathers	Light royal blue spotted batik	1½" x 6" (3.8 x 15.2cm)	Royal blue (#232)
Y. Long tail feathers	Aqua and blue leaf patterned batik	Various sizes	Stone blue (#903)
aa. Side black border pieces (cut 2)	Black batik	3¾" x 4" (9.5 x 10.2cm)	Optional
bb. Side chicken wire border pieces (cut 2)	Chicken wire pattern	3¾" x 12¼" (9.5 x 31.1cm)	Optional
cc. Top and bottom black border pieces (cut 2)	Black batik	3¾" x 18¾" (9.5 x 47.6cm)	Optional

*Note: Gütermann sponsored this design by donating all the threads used to create the example art quilt.

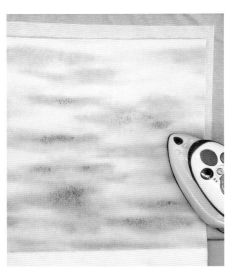

1. Start making your quilt sandwich. Iron or spray together the backing and batting; either by ironing together if using fusible fleece or using quilt basting spray if using a thin cotton batting. (See Start Making the Quilt Sandwich on page 34 for additional tips.) With rotary cutter and ruler, trim the quilt sandwich to 12" x 16" (30.5 x 40.6cm).

2. Choose your fabrics, press them with spray sizing (optional), and back them with iron-on adhesive. Do not back the border fabrics (aa, bb, and cc). Press the background sky fabric (A) onto the top of the fuzzy batting layer of the batting and backing set.

3. Topstitch across the sky in wavy, cloud-like lines.

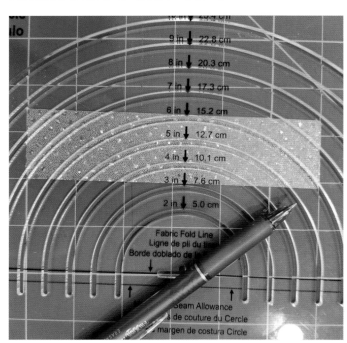

4. Use a circular ruler or the edge of a 6" (15.2cm) plate and an erasable marker to draw an arc along the top of the gold sun fabric strip (B). Cut this piece along the line to create the sun shape.

5. Fussy cut some small plants and grasses from the plant and grass fabric pieces (C, D, and E).

6. Add the sun shape on top of the bottom right of the stitched-down sky and add the fussy-cut flower (D) and peach grass (E) as desired. Use a rotary cutter to cut a rolling edge along the top of the sand fabric piece (F), then place it down on the bottom of the batting and backing set, slightly overlapping the plants, sun, and sky pieces.

7. Press these pieces down to the art quilt surface, using parchment paper under the iron to protect the gem-covered gold sun fabric. Only press down the bottom of the peach grass for now, leaving the top free. **Note:** Don't panic when you see that the tan does not cover the lower edge of the batting. You'll fill this space with groundcover in later steps.

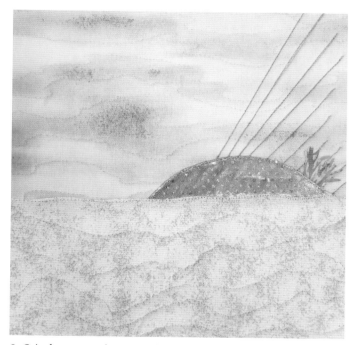

8. Use an erasable marker and a ruler to draw about 10 sun rays extending from the top right edge of the sun. Note that only pressing down the bottom of the peach grass lets you easily maneuver around it to draw and then stitch the gold sun rays. You can even temporarily use a small piece of masking tape to hold the piece out of the way if you need to.

9. Stitch across the top edge of the sun and back and forth along the sun ray lines with gold thread. Then stitch wavy lines across the sand with light tan thread. Set the art quilt surface aside for now.

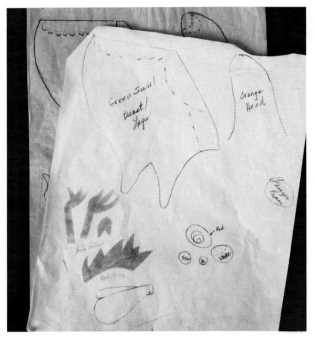

10. Trace the rooster template pieces onto freezer paper. See templates on page 140. Use paper scissors to roughly cut out each template piece. Also trace the rooster's head and body on parchment paper to prepare for the parchment paper collaging in steps 13–19. **Note:** The templates shown in these photos are the original hand-drawn versions.

11. Place a piece of parchment paper on your ironing board, then place your rooster eye and body fabric pieces (J–P and S) adhesive side down on top of the parchment paper. Add the freezer paper template pieces on top of the correct fabric for each piece with the waxy side down. Press all the template pieces with the corresponding fabrics. Once they are cool, fussy cut each template/fabric set and remove the freezer paper. Cut an extra smaller white circle from the scrap of the white fabric (M). This will be the catchlight in the center of the eye. See Using Freezer Paper Templates on page 55.

12. Begin by collaging the eye. Press the larger white eye piece (M) onto a piece of parchment paper. Then press on the remaining eye pieces in this order, as shown: the red piece (J), the yellow piece (L), the black piece (K), and the extra white circle cut from the white scrap fabric (M). Press the whole thing together. Once it has cooled, peel the eye off the parchment paper.

13. Collage the head. Press the head fabric piece (P) onto a piece of parchment paper. Then add the comb and wattle pieces (O) and the beak (N) and press. Add the completed eye on top, overlapping all the pieces where they meet. Press. **Note:** This photo shows how you can construct the piece directly on top of your parchment paper sketch.

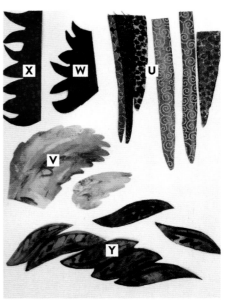

14. Fussy cut the tops and bottoms of the upper and lower neck ruff fabric pieces (Q and R) with scallops. Arrange the pieces at the bottom of the rooster's neck with the upper piece (Q) overlapping the lower piece (R). Press both down, leaving the bottom of the lower piece (R) unpressed. Use an erasable pen to draw the line of the neck on both sides of the neck ruff, then trim off the excess fabric.

15. Tuck the top edge of the chest and leg piece (S) under the unpressed bottom of the lower neck piece. Then tuck the feet pieces (N) under the bottom edges of the legs. Press down only the lower part of the body, the legs, and the feet. Do not press down the lower neck ruff yet.

16. Cut the wing pieces. Fussy cut the upper wing fabric piece (T, not shown in this photo) into an oval by trimming off the corners of the square. Fussy or rotary cut the lower wing fabric pieces (U) into long pointed feathers. Fussy cut the top back feathers (V) with scallops on the top and right edge. Fussy cut the first and second row tail feathers (W and X) with an edge of short feathery points. Finally, fussy cut the long tail feathers (Y) into pointed ovals.

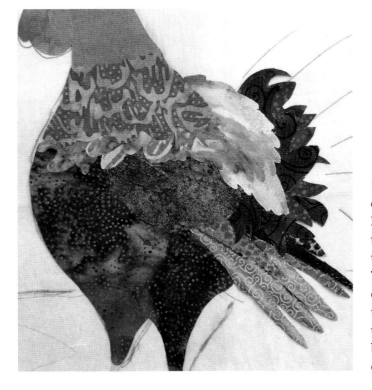

17. Lift up the right edge of lower neck ruff and tuck the top edge of the upper wing (T) in between the ruff and the body. Insert the lower wing feathers (U) under the bottom edge of the upper wing oval, but on top of the rooster's body. Add the top back feathers and the first and second row tail feathers. The first and second row tail feathers should overlap each other and the lower wing feathers. They should be beneath the upper wing. The top back feathers should overlap the upper wing and the first and second tail feather layers but be beneath the neck ruff. Press everything except the right edges of the wing and tail pieces.

18. Arrange the remaining long tail feathers (Y) as desired, layering them and tucking them in under the right edges of the long lower wing feathers and the second row tail feathers. Be careful to keep the tail short enough that it won't extend off the edge of the art quilt or cover the sun.

19. Press everything in place. Once the completed rooster is cool, peel the entire piece off the parchment paper and set it aside.

20. Fussy cut the top edges of all the ground cover fabric pieces (G–I). Try to think organically to convey earth and plant textures.

21. Arrange these pieces together as desired, using the parchment paper sketch as a placement guide. Do not press yet.

22. Slip a strip of parchment paper between the brown and peach strips and underneath the green strips. Press at the same time to create two separate strips. Peel each off the parchment paper and set both strips aside.

23. Press the combined brown and peach strip piece to the bottom of the art quilt, on top of the tan sand.

24. Stitch down the top edges of combined brown and peach strip piece using matching threads. Thread paint and fussy stitch around and through these fabrics. Then press the combined green strip on the bottom of the brown and peach layer. Stitch down this green layer, following the outer edge and creating grassy spikes.

25. Press the completed rooster on top of the stitched-down scene.

26. Stitch around the outside edges of the rooster using matching threads. Also use matching threads to add details in the middle of the neck, wattle, body, and wing pieces. Try to replicate a rooster's feathery texture.

27. If desired, fussy cut small dots from the brown pebble fabric scrap pieces (G) and scatter them around the rooster's feet to look like chicken feed. Press them down.

28. Press the entire scene with moisture, then square up the sides of the piece with a ruler and rotary cutter and set aside. Sew one 3¾" edge of each short black border piece to the 3¾" edge of each chicken wire border piece. Sew these border strips to the right and left sides of the art quilt, with the chicken wire fabric pieces on top. Sew the top and bottom black border pieces to the top and bottom of the art quilt. Press the seams flat toward the outside edges and square the whole quilt top to 18½" x 22½" (47 x 57.2cm). See Set into a Border on page 43.

29. Use a large glue stick to wrap a stretched art canvas with the completed art quilt and border fabric piece, centering the art quilt scene over the stretched art canvas. See Covering a Stretched Art Canvas on page 44.

Templates

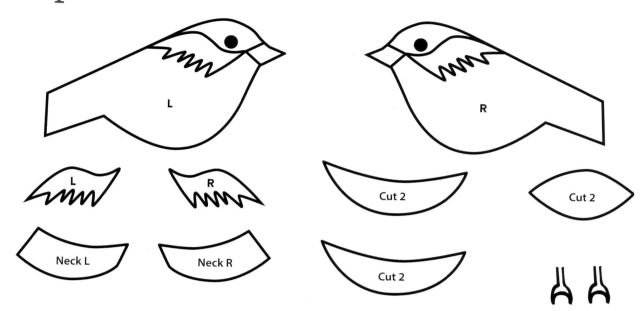

L

R

L R

Cut 2

Cut 2

Neck L Neck R

Cut 2

The Chickadees templates

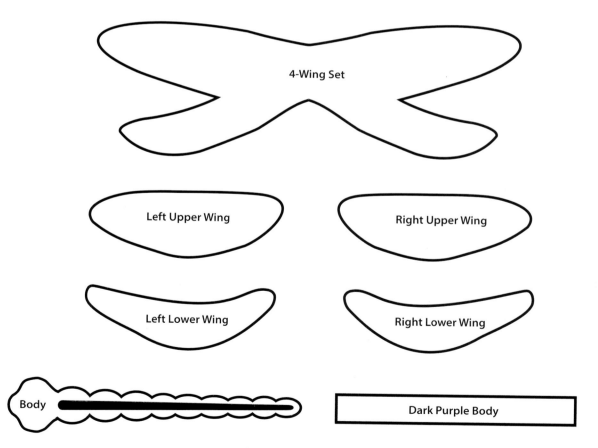

4-Wing Set

Left Upper Wing

Right Upper Wing

Left Lower Wing

Right Lower Wing

Body

Dark Purple Body

Miss Dragonfly templates

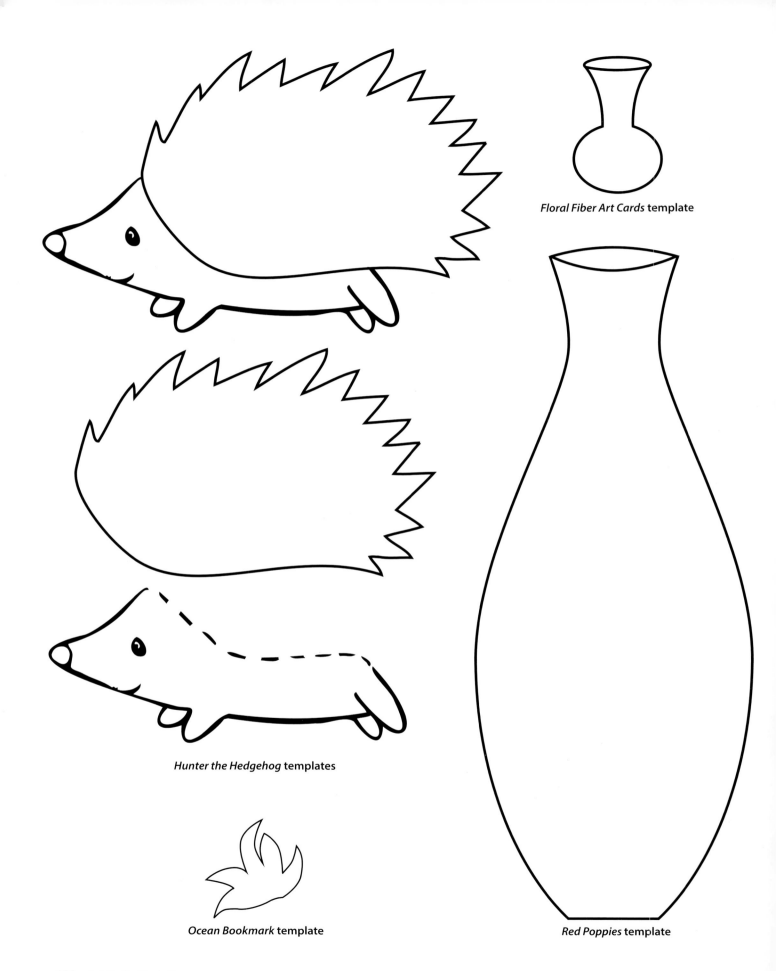

Floral Fiber Art Cards **template**

Hunter the Hedgehog **templates**

Ocean Bookmark **template**

Red Poppies **template**

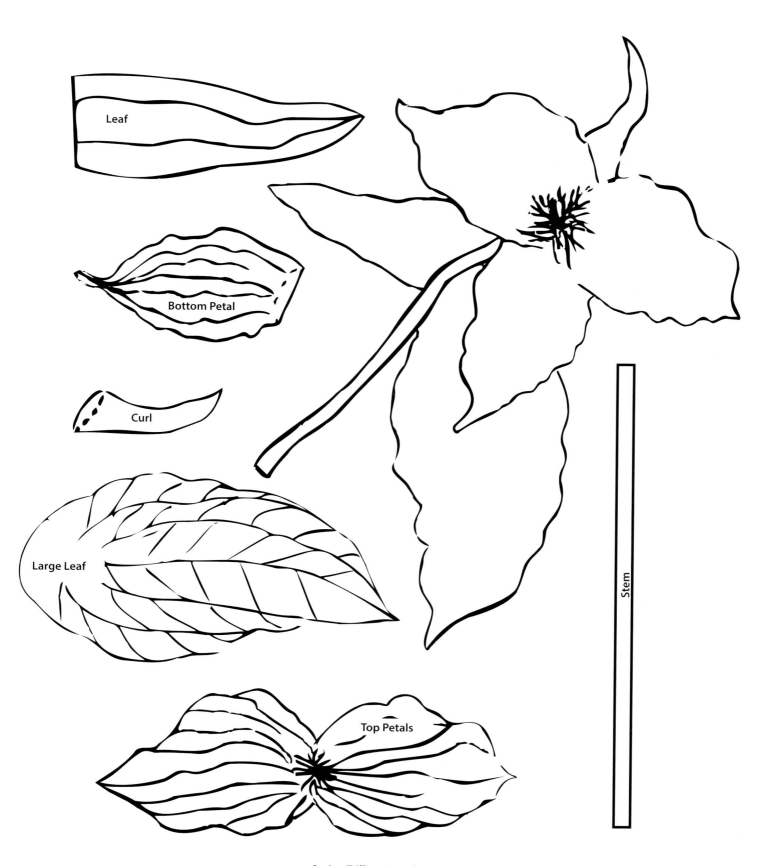

Leaf

Bottom Petal

Curl

Large Leaf

Top Petals

Stem

Spring Trillium templates

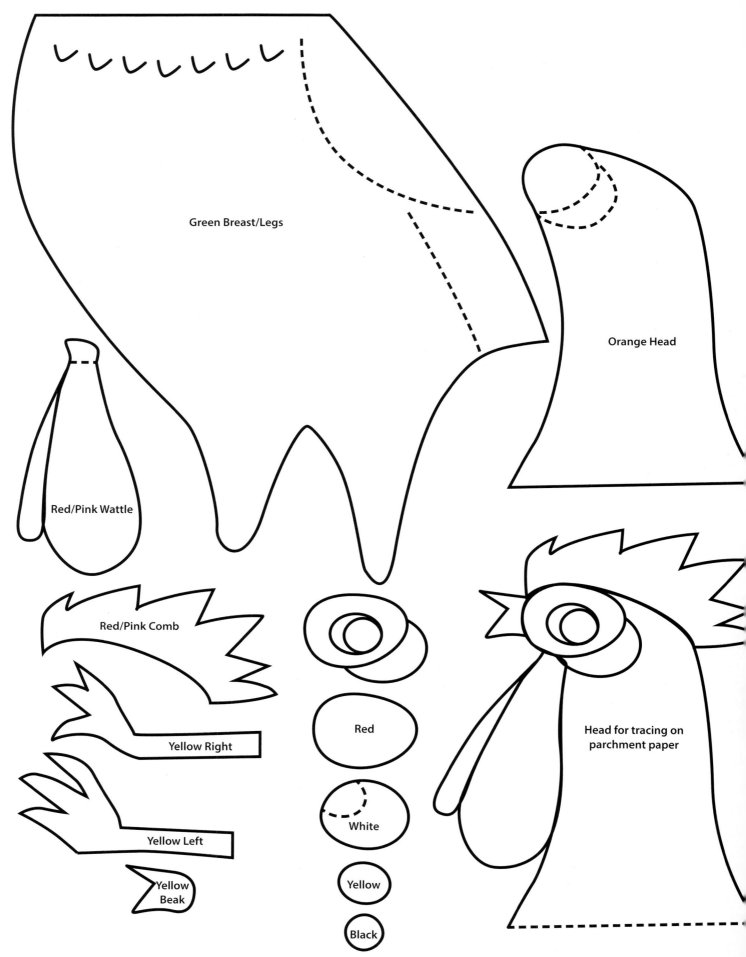

Green Breast/Legs

Orange Head

Red/Pink Wattle

Red/Pink Comb

Yellow Right

Yellow Left

Yellow Beak

Red

White

Yellow

Black

Head for tracing on parchment paper

Rise & Shine! templates

Index

About the Author

Dr. Susan Jenae Kruszynski lives in Muskegon, Michigan, and is an award-winning art quilt designer, teacher, and gallery artist. At the age of 8, Susan's maternal grandmother handed her an embroidery project. That initiated her over 50-year experimentation with fabrics to produce colorful artistic creations. She began landscape fiber art design with collage art quilts in 2014. A native of Michigan, her works are often inspired by the trees and woodlands along the Lake Michigan shoreline.

Susan currently divides her time between creating original collaged art quilt designs, teaching art quilting classes in and around the state of Michigan, marketing this fiber art at shows and exhibitions, and running her Quilting Fabrics in Time business; she only just recently retired as a literacy specialist at Muskegon Community College. She enjoys visiting her three daughters and their families, including her grandpets, in Dallas, Texas. Susan uses her 40+ years of K-College level teaching experiences and her PhD in education to provide fun and easy learning experiences in classes and with online instruction. Her art quilts range in sizes from 3" x 5" (7.6 x 12.7cm) to 40" x 60" (101 x 152cm).

By hand cutting, collaging, pressing, and machine stitching pieces of fabric together, Susan creates art quilts that look like paintings. With this book, she hopes to add value to her readers' lives by teaching the principles for creating collage art quilts. She's hoping that with her help, you can make one or more projects from this book. You may pick up some tips that will supplement your current quilting skills. And, best of all, perhaps you will experience the joy of art quilting and feel emboldened and secure enough to create additional art quilts of your own.

For more inspiration from Susan's work, be sure to check out her first book, *Starter Guide to Creating Art Quilts*, released in 2021. Also, feel free to view more of her artwork in the gallery on her website.

Awards

- Grand Rapids ArtPrize Nine 2017 (TOP 25), *Reaching Upward*; Eleven 28" x 36" (71.1 x 91.4cm) story panels
- Michigan Education Association (MEA) Art Acquisitions Purchase Exhibition, *Kruszing Thru the Seasons*; 12" x 42" (30.5 x 106.7cm) in 2018 and *Teal Trees*; 24" x 36" (61 x 91.4cm) in 2019 (Jurors' Choice Award and Purchase Awards)
- Grand Haven Lighthouse Quilt Guild Show, 1st Place, *Teal Trees*; 24" x 36" (61 x 91.4cm) in 2018 and *Resilience #1*; 40" x 60" (101.6 x 152.4cm) in 2019
- Michigan Education Association (MEA) Art Acquisition and Purchase Exhibition Brochure cover design for 2020—*Teal Trees*; 24" x 36" (61 x 91.4cm)

Galleries

- Gallery Uptown—Grand Haven, Michigan
- Muskegon Museum of Art—Muskegon, Michigan
- Newaygo County Council for the Arts, Artsplace—Fremont, Michigan

Media

- Website—*www.quiltingfabricsintime.com*
- Facebook—Quilting Fabrics in Time—*https://www.facebook.com/Quilting-Fabrics-In-Time-1694599947516014*
- Instagram—*www.instagram.com/quiltingfabricsintime*
- Etsy—*https://www.etsy.com/shop/ArtQuiltsbySusan*